Cambridge Elements

Elements in Forensic Linguistics
edited by
Tim Grant
Aston University
Tammy Gales
Hofstra University

FORENSIC LINGUISTICS IN INDONESIA

Origins, Progress, and Prospects

R. Dian Dia-an Muniroh
Universitas Pendidikan Indonesia

E. Aminudin Aziz
Universitas Pendidikan Indonesia

CAMBRIDGE
UNIVERSITY PRESS

Shaftesbury Road, Cambridge CB2 8EA, United Kingdom

One Liberty Plaza, 20th Floor, New York, NY 10006, USA

477 Williamstown Road, Port Melbourne, VIC 3207, Australia

314–321, 3rd Floor, Plot 3, Splendor Forum, Jasola District Centre,
New Delhi – 110025, India

Cambridge University Press is part of Cambridge University Press & Assessment,
a department of the University of Cambridge.

We share the University's mission to contribute to society through the pursuit of
education, learning and research at the highest international levels of excellence.

www.cambridge.org
Information on this title: www.cambridge.org/9781009474405

DOI: 10.1017/9781009474412

First published 2026

A catalogue record for this publication is available from the British Library

A Cataloging-in-Publication data record for this Element is available from
the Library of Congress

ISBN 978-1-009-47440-5 Hardback
ISBN 978-1-009-47439-9 Paperback
ISSN 2634-7334 (online)
ISSN 2634-7326 (print)

Forensic Linguistics in Indonesia

Origins, Progress, and Prospects

Elements in Forensic Linguistics

DOI: 10.1017/9781009474412
First published online: April 2026

R. Dian Dia-an Muniroh
Universitas Pendidikan Indonesia

E. Aminudin Aziz
Universitas Pendidikan Indonesia

Author for correspondence: R. Dian Dia-an Muniroh, ddmuniroh@upi.edu

Abstract: This Element examines the origins, development, and prospects of forensic linguistics in Indonesia, drawing on a survey of 53 participants and a systematic review of studies from 2011 to 2023. Emerging from early language-related cases in the Old Order era and initially driven by scholars trained abroad, the field has grown through research, collaboration, and academic integration. Key topics include justice sector needs, linguistic diversity, standardization, and institutional strengthening. Despite limited capacity-building, training initiatives have enhanced the field's visibility. The Element outlines challenges and opportunities for advancing forensic linguistics' role in legal reform and fair justice, making it a valuable reference for scholars and practitioners.

Keywords: forensic linguistics, Indonesia, language as evidence, multilingual justice, investigative interviewing

ISBNs: 9781009474405 (HB), 9781009474399 (PB), 9781009474412 (OC)
ISSNs: 2634-7334 (online), 2634-7326 (print)

Contents

Series Preface

The Elements in Forensic Linguistics series from Cambridge University Press Publishes across four main topic areas (1) investigative and forensic text analysis; (2) the study of spoken linguistic practices in legal contexts; (3) the linguistic analysis of written legal texts; and (4) explorations of the origins, development and scope of the field in various countries and regions.

Forensic Linguistics in Indonesia: Origins, Progress, and Prospects by R. Dian Dia-an Muniroh and E. Aminudin Aziz, is the fifth Origins Element in the series focusing on diverse forensic linguistic development in the Philippines, Australia, China and Southern Africa. In providing this Element the authors bring to attention to a further global south nation where the discipline has taken hold and is developing fast.

This Element traces the history of language evidence in the Indonesian justice system back to the 1950's and then brings it forward to its institutionalised development through both the higher education systems and through governmental intervention and support to a degree that has not been observed in the previous Origins Elements. The systematic literature review of research evidences the breadth of interests across the subdisciplines of forensic linguistics with strongest showing in the area of language as evidence and the section on practice shows how language expertise can and is making impact in cases including in court.

Overall, this is a valuable contribution to the Elements series, both itself by providing a fascinating insight into Indonesian forensic and legal linguistics, and also in terms of contrasts with the other countries and jurisdictions already covered in the growing *Origins* subseries. We look forward to more of the same.

Tim Grant

Series Editor

1 Introduction

1.1 Introducing the Element

In this Element, we provide a comprehensive discussion on forensic linguistics, beginning with its definition and conceptual scope. Our exploration then extends to the historical development of forensic linguistics in Indonesia, tracing its origins, early influences, key milestones, first encounters with the field, and its defining characteristics within the Indonesian context. Beyond its historical evolution, we examine forensic linguistic research in Indonesia, incorporating linguistic theories and concepts, methodological approaches, interdisciplinary connections, and collaborative efforts. We also discuss forensic linguistic practices in Indonesia, covering the role of language experts, the preparation of expert reports, analytical models, and ethical considerations. In the conclusion, we present summary, identify key challenges, and outline future directions.

To enrich our analysis, we integrate findings from a purposefully administered survey which was conducted in Indonesian, capturing the perspectives of fifty-three forensic linguistics researchers and practitioners. This survey provides empirical evidence and diverse insights, offering an emic perspective on the definition and scope of forensic linguistics in Indonesia. Additionally, it reveals how academics and practitioners first encountered the field. To support our discussion, we conducted a literature search using Publish or Perish software and Google Scholar, analyzing publications from 2011 to 2023 with five keywords: forensic linguistics, language and law, language as evidence, legal linguistics, and Indonesia. This period was chosen because 2011 marks a significant milestone in the development of forensic linguistics in Indonesia.

In this section, we embark on an in-depth examination of forensic linguistics, the Indonesian legal system, and the sociocultural challenges unique to the region. Recognizing Indonesia's diverse sociolinguistic landscape, we aim to unravel the complex interplay between language, culture, and the legal domain.

1.2 Definition and Overview of Forensic Linguistics

This Element explores the applications of linguistic analysis in law and crime in Indonesia, defining forensic linguistics through global perspectives from foundational works such as Svartvik (1968), Shuy (2006), Grant and MacLeod (2020), alongside insights from Indonesian academics and practitioners obtained through a purposeful survey. In Indonesia, participants largely view forensic linguistics as applied linguistics, reflecting earlier global definitions but showing limited awareness of recent distinctions between forensic and legal linguistics (see e.g. Guillén-Nieto & Stein, 2022; Longhi & Makouar, 2025; Wright & Picornell, 2024). Future development should integrate interdisciplinary knowledge and methods to enhance the role of language analysis in justice processes. Influential contributions by scholars such as O'Barr, Solan, Le Cheng, Šarčević, and Goźdź-Roszkowski, covering legal discourse, statutory interpretation, multilingual legal systems, and interdisciplinary law-language studies, remain acknowledged. This section addresses four aspects: historical and global definitions, disciplinary distinctions, Indonesian perspectives, and the working definition in Indonesia.

1.2.1 Historical and Global Definitions

All literature acknowledges and agrees that the earliest term related to the study of language as applied in law and criminal contexts is forensic linguistics, introduced by Jan Svartvik in 1968 in his book, *The Evans Statements: A Case for Forensic Linguistics* (e.g. Ariani et al., 2014; Perkins, 2021). This marked the initial instance of applying contemporary technical linguistic knowledge scientifically. Although Philbrick used the term "Forensic English" in his 1949 book titled *Language and the Law: The Semantics of Forensic English*, it did not become widely adopted (Coulthard & Johnson, 2010).

In the early 1990s, experts such as Levi (1994), Gibbons (1999), and Kniffka (1996) considered forensic linguistics a subset of the broader field of language and law.[1] While language and the law is a broader interdisciplinary field that investigates how language functions in legal contexts including legal language, language rights, and courtroom discourse, forensic linguistics refers more narrowly to the scientific analysis of language as evidence in legal and investigative contexts. Levi (1994), in her extensive bibliography on language and the law, divides the field into three main categories: spoken language in legal settings, language as a subject of the law, and the written language of the law, with an additional applied category of forensic linguistics. Similarly, Gibbons (1999) categorizes the field in his edited book based on the topics of the papers: language constructing law, language and disadvantage before the law, and forensic linguistics. Aligning with both experts, Kniffka (1996, p. 22) states that the "mother-field" of forensic linguistics is language and the law. At the same time, he acknowledges that forensic linguistics also functions as a form of applied linguistic expertise, particularly in legal and judicial contexts. As he explains, "forensic linguistics involves basic and applied research in the area of linguistic expert testimony in court" (Kniffka, 1996, p. 31).

In contrast, other scholars view forensic linguistics exclusively as a branch of applied linguistics. Kurzon (1997), for example, noted that forensic linguistics involves the applied use of certain linguistic approaches to problems that may arise in the judicial, especially criminal process. Much of the work deals with voice recognition, which may be included under applied phonology (Kurzon, 1997, p. 121). Shuy viewed forensic linguistics as a branch of applied linguistics: "Forensic linguistics is, after all, primarily the study and use of linguistic tools in the legal context" (2017, p. 639). McMenamin (2002) also defined forensic linguistics as applied linguistics: "Forensic linguistics is the scientific study of language as applied to forensic purposes and contexts." McMenamin

---

[1] The phrase "language and law" was first introduced by Peter M. Tiersma to encompass the diverse forms and branches of forensic linguistic work worldwide (Kniffka, 2015; Tiersma, 1993).

further acknowledged that other terms coexist with forensic linguistics, such as legal linguistics or language and the law: "the interconnection of linguistics and other disciplines, including law (Tiersma, 2008), is the emergence of forensic linguistics, also known more generally as legal linguistics or language and the law" (McMenamin, 2002) (see Alduais et al., 2023; Olsson & Luchjenbroers, 2014).

When viewed as a branch of applied linguistics, it is understandable that during its development, some people use and accept the term "forensic linguistics" in a very broad sense. This broader interpretation encompasses any use of linguistic tools in a legal context, not limited solely to the provision of linguistic evidence. Consequently, they also view forensic linguistics as nearly synonymous with "language and the law." However, while both fields overlap particularly in areas like legal discourse and courtroom interaction, language and the law is a broader interdisciplinary field, whereas forensic linguistics refers more narrowly to the scientific analysis of language as evidence in legal and investigative settings. The following paragraph offers an alternative perspective, framing forensic linguistics as encompassing both broad and narrow definitions in terms of its scope.

Other experts define forensic linguistics both broadly and narrowly. The term has come to encompass all areas defined by Coulthard and Johnson (2010) and Coulthard, May, and Sousa-Silva (2010): the written language of the law, spoken interaction in legal contexts, and language as evidence, while the narrow definition restricts the discipline to language as evidence alone. Gibbons (1999) defines forensic linguistics in the strict sense as "the field of the provision of linguistic evidence." The broad coverage of forensic linguistics is also highlighted by Hutton (2009, p. xi):

> Forensic linguistics is concerned with how linguistics can be applied in an evidential or expert witness capacity, or in defense of the language rights of groups disadvantaged by the legal process's language culture. It deals with issues such as legal interpreting and translation; the comprehensibility of legal documents, jury instructions, and police communication with suspects and the general public; issues of age, gender, and race within the discourse of the legal system; discourse analysis of the language of judges; plagiarism; and the authenticity of documents.

Olsson and Luchjenbroers (2014) describe forensic linguistics in the broadest sense as the interface between language, crime, and law, encompassing law enforcement, judicial matters, legislation, disputes or proceedings in law, and even disputes potentially involving some infraction of the law or a necessity to seek a legal remedy.

In the 1990s, forensic linguists formed the International Association of Forensic Linguists (IAFL), and the information on its website also uses a broad definition: "In its broadest sense, 'forensic linguistics' covers all areas where law and language intersect: language and law, language in the legal process, language as evidence, research, and teaching" (https://www.iafl.org/forensic-linguistics, accessed 2020). This content is still maintained after the name changed to the International Association for Forensic and Legal Linguistics (IAFLL) (https://iafll.org/forensic-linguistics/, accessed June 6, 2024).

As Alduais (2023) notes, "Broadly defined and better known as "language and law," forensic linguistics is the application of linguistic theory and method to any point where there is an interface between language and the law" (Macleod & Wright, 2020, p. 360). It includes language analysis and study as applied to legal settings (Kniffka, 2007), the study of courtroom discourse (Tiersma, 1999; Yi, 2024), legal interpretation and translation (Berk-Seligson, 2012; Ng, 2023), the readability and comprehensibility of legal documents and jury instructions (Tracy, 2024), police caution comprehensibility to suspects (Svennevig et al., 2024), and linguistic minorities in the legal process (Eades, 1994; Eades & Pavlenko, 2016; Pavlenko, 2024). For further definitions of forensic linguistics, see also Ariani et al. (2014).

It is important to mention the area of legal discourse, a significant branch of language and law. It operates as an intersemiotic process linking discourse, law, and society. It covers written forms like legislation, spoken forms such as courtroom interaction, and nonverbal elements including physical evidence and courtroom layout (Cheng & Danesi, 2019). This perspective highlights the interplay of legal texts and other sign systems within cultural, social, economic, and human rights contexts. Scholarship in this area is featured in *The International Journal of Legal Discourse* and showcases interdisciplinary research connecting law, linguistics, semiotics, politics, sociology, and psychology.

Among the various perspectives on forensic linguistics, a unifying thread across definitions is its applied nature and the interdisciplinary domains it encompasses. This framework is particularly useful for discussing forensic linguistics in the Indonesian context. Additionally, a significant perspective comes from Grant and MacLeod (2020), who highlight a critical dimension of the field: its role in enhancing the delivery of justice through linguistic analysis. This definition not only complements the common applied focus but also underscores the importance of addressing justice-related issues. This critical dimension is essential for ensuring that forensic linguistics contributes meaningfully to legal proceedings and promotes equitable access to justice.

1.2.2 Distinction between Legal Linguistics and Forensic Linguistics

While McMenamin (2002) acknowledged the coexistence of the terms *legal linguistics* and *forensic linguistics*, recent scholarship has introduced a clear distinction between the two entities. Guillén-Nieto and Stein (2022) argue that legal linguistics primarily addresses the theoretical and systemic aspects of language within the legal domain, such as legislative drafting and legal interpretation. In contrast, forensic linguistics focuses on the practical application of linguistic analysis to legal evidence, often in adversarial contexts. They describe forensic linguistics as

> [t]he use of evidence from language use, based on records or "texts," or "traces" – not as live substance, but as vestiges of the use of language, of communication or speech acts that took place in the past, however medially constituted, spoken, written, digital, in connection with the resolution of crime. (Guillén-Nieto & Stein, 2022, p. 4)

Additionally, they elaborate:

> The legal linguist is a theoretician, but the forensic linguist has the practical task of having to act, to appear at court, know the rules of conducting and executing this part of the law, different in different legal cultures [...] and also acquire a rhetoric for presenting evidence at court. (Guillén-Nieto & Stein, 2022, p. 16)

This distinction reflects the differing emphases within language and law. Legal linguistics focuses on theoretical and analytical frameworks for language in legal contexts, such as courtroom interaction, legislative drafting, and legal reasoning. Forensic linguistics, in its narrower sense, applies linguistic analysis to legal evidence, including authorship attribution, speaker profiling, and contested meanings. The aim is not to set rigid boundaries but to show how one is more academic and interpretive, the other more investigative and case-specific.

This differentiation is also reflected in the International Association of Forensic and Legal Linguistics (IAFLL), formerly known as the International Association of Forensic Linguists (IAFL). The rebranding highlights the multi-faceted intersections of language and law and the diverse roles involved in language-related legal contexts. IAFLL's tagline, "Bringing together the global forensic and legal linguistic community," reflects its commitment to fostering collaboration across these domains. According to the IAFLL Constitution (Article 1), the organization's primary goal is to enhance the functioning of legal systems worldwide by promoting a deeper understanding of the interactions between language and law (IAFLL, https://iafll.org/constitution/).

1.2.3 Emic Perspectives from Indonesian Scholars and Practitioners

In Indonesia, scholars' and practitioners' understanding of forensic linguistics tends to align with earlier global definitions. However, the distinction between legal linguistics and forensic linguistics is less pronounced. Notably, the term *linguistik hukum* (ENG legal linguistics) was absent from participants' responses, indicating a limited awareness of its distinction from forensic linguistics, which is a relatively new field in Indonesia. This observation emerged from our survey, which was carried out in Indonesian, and assessed participants' understanding of forensic linguistics. Their exposure to the field varied: less than 1 year (17%), 1–5 years (42%), 5–10 years (25%), and more than 10 years (17%). Participants generally defined forensic linguistics in three main ways:

1) As the application of linguistic theory and methods to legal contexts (see Excerpt #1).

   Excerpt #1
   IND: *Penerapan ilmu bahasa pada ranah hukum.* (Partisipan #8)[2]
   ENG: The application of linguistics in the field of law. (Participant #8)

2) As a broad term encompassing the application of linguistics to legal contexts, as well as a narrower focus on language as evidence (see Excerpts #2 and #3).

   Excerpt #2
   IND: *Penerapan linguistik dalam ranah hukum, baik dalam analisis alat bukti hukum, produk hukum, maupun proses hukum.* (Partisipan #5)
   ENG: The application of linguistics in the field of law, including the analysis of legal evidence, legal products, and legal processes. (Participant #5)
   Excerpt #3
   IND: *Cabang ilmu bahasa yang menelaah seluk beluk bahasa sebagai bukti, baik itu dalam rangka profiling, pengawasan, intelijen, maupun penegakan hukum.* (Partisipan #20)
   ENG: A branch of linguistics that examines the intricacies of language as evidence, whether for profiling, surveillance, intelligence, or law enforcement. (Participant #20)

3) As a discipline with a justice-oriented focus, emphasizing its role in enforcing law (see Excerpt #4).

---

[2] Original examples are in Indonesian (indicated by *IND*). English translations follow each example (indicated by ENG).

Excerpt #4

IND: *Pengaplikasian ilmu linguistik dalam data bahasa untuk membantu dalam penegakan hukum.* (Partisipan #3)

ENG: The application of linguistic science to language data to assist in law enforcement. (Participant #3)

1.2.4 Working Definition of Forensic Linguistics

Informed by global scholarly perspectives and insights from participant responses, this Element adopts a comprehensive view of forensic linguistics as an applied discipline. It bridges interdisciplinary areas, encompasses both broad and narrow scopes, and emphasizes critical, justice-oriented dimensions. This approach does not disregard the distinction between forensic linguistics and legal linguistics but reflects the emic perspectives of participants, which is a central objective of this work.

Accordingly, forensic linguistics for Indonesian context is defined as the interdisciplinary scientific study of language applied in legal and investigative contexts, with a justice-oriented focus. It includes linguistic evidence analysis, examination of spoken and written legal communication, linguistic disadvantages in legal processes, legal document analysis, forensic linguistics literacy education, all as efforts to promote equitable legal processes. This operational definition integrates established global traditions with Indonesia's unique multilingual and multicultural landscape, addressing its specific legal and sociolinguistic challenges.

Furthermore, as with linguistics as a whole, which traditionally encompasses two major avenues – research and practice (Shuy, 2017; Tayebi & Coulthard, 2022) – this Element explores both the research and practical applications of forensic linguistics within the Indonesian context (see Section 3 and Section 4). The following section elaborates Indonesia's legal landscape and sociocultural contexts.

1.3 Indonesia's Legal Landscape and Sociocultural Contexts

The study of forensic linguistics shows strong potential in Indonesia, reflected in increasing collaboration between law enforcement apparatus and linguistic experts in investigative interviewing, expert testimony, and high-profile cases (see Sections 2.1.2 and 4.1). Such engagement can enhance cultural sensitivity, communication, decision-making, and legal processes, contributing to a more just legal system.

Essentially, language underpins all legal matters in a state governed by law, as recognized in Article 1 Section (3) of the 1945 Constitution. From drafting legislation to presenting evidence, the legal system is language-centric, making linguistic expertise essential (Shuy, 2008). In this regard, reliable analysis requires high awareness of language's role and integrating language considerations into legal processes (Shuy, 2006, 2008).

This section outlines Indonesia's legal, criminal, and sociocultural contexts, examining how they shape the development of forensic linguistics and how linguistic expertise can address legal challenges. It establishes the field's relevance and potential to improve legal processes and outcomes in Indonesia.

1.3.1 Indonesia's Legal System

Indonesia's legal system is both diverse and complex, reflecting its rich history with multiple legal traditions. As a former Dutch colony, Indonesia primarily inherited the Dutch Civil Law system, which serves as the foundation of its legal framework. However, Indonesia's legal landscape also integrates two other significant traditions: the *hukum adat* (customary legal system) and the religious legal system grounded in Islamic Sharia law (Butt & Lindsey, 2018; Wardhani et al., 2022). This coexistence of multiple legal systems is referred to as legal pluralism (Isra & Tegnan, 2021; Lukito, 2012), a condition in which a population adheres to more than one body of law (Woodman, 1999). The application of civil law, customary law, or Islamic law depends on the specific case and the cultural or religious backgrounds of the people involved.

Over time, Indonesia has adapted its colonial-era laws to align more closely with national values and societal needs, often incorporating *adat* (customary) and Islamic principles where appropriate. Notably, the interplay of these three legal systems predates Indonesia's independence, reflecting centuries of legal evolution. In this complex legal framework, linguistic analysis contributes to enhance transparency, fairness, and effectiveness within the legal system. Its contribution might include clarifying legal ambiguities in statutory writing (e.g. Rifai, 2020; Solan, 2010), examining the relationship between linguistic structures and legal interpretation (e.g. Solan, 2005; Tiersma, 2008) and promoting legal awareness and literacy (cf. Toan, 2024).

The following sections examine the distinctive features and contemporary applications of civil law, customary law, and Islamic law within Indonesia's legal framework. Additionally, they highlight the significant and multifaceted roles of language analysis in enhancing the delivery of justice and ensuring fairness across these interconnected legal systems.

Civil Law System

The civil legal system in general exhibits distinctive characteristics, namely (1) the law is predominantly written and organized in the form of legal codes, statutes, and regulations; and (2) unlike the common law system based on the doctrine of *stare decisis*, where judges are bound by precedents, the Indonesian legal system gives judges more flexibility in guiding, influencing, and deciding cases through an inquisitorial approach. In this regard, judges play a significant role in the judicial process (Budiono et al., 2023; Butt & Lindsey, 2018). Yet, jurisprudence can still be considered by judges in deciding cases.

Indonesia's legal system follows a hierarchical structure as stipulated in Article 7 Section (1) Law Number 12 of 2011 on the Establishment of Laws and Regulations, with the 1945 Constitution of the Republic of Indonesia holding the highest position. This is followed respectively by the *Ketetapan Majelis Permusyawaratan Rakyat* (ENG Decree of People's Consultative Assembly), statute/legislation, government regulations in lieu of laws, government regulation, presidential regulation, provincial regulation, and regency or municipality regulations.

The court system in Indonesia has three main tiers: District Courts (the first instance of appeal in each regional area), High Courts (courts of appeal in each province), and the Supreme Court (the highest judicial institution at the national level). The Supreme Court oversees four distinct court jurisdictions: general courts, administrative courts, religious courts, and military courts (see Figure 1).

General courts handle a wide range of civil and criminal cases. Within the general court system, there are also several special courts that have the authority to investigate, prosecute, and rule on specific types of cases. These include, among others, the Industrial Relations Dispute Court, Commercial Court, and Corruption Court (Butt & Lindsey, 2018; Crouch, 2019). The creation of specialized courts after authoritarian rule has been a notable aspect of Indonesia's court reform efforts. Crouch (2021, p. 2) noted: "The trend towards judicial specialization can be found across jurisdictions in Asia, although the Indonesian case is remarkable in the scale and breadth of areas of specialization."

Administrative courts have the jurisdiction to resolve disputes arising from decisions made by government officials and administrative bodies. Religious courts have the authority to settle issues within the Muslim community, such as those related to marriage, inheritance, wills, grants, *waqf* (ENG Islamic endowments), *zakat* (ENG charitable donations), *infaq* (ENG voluntary contributions),

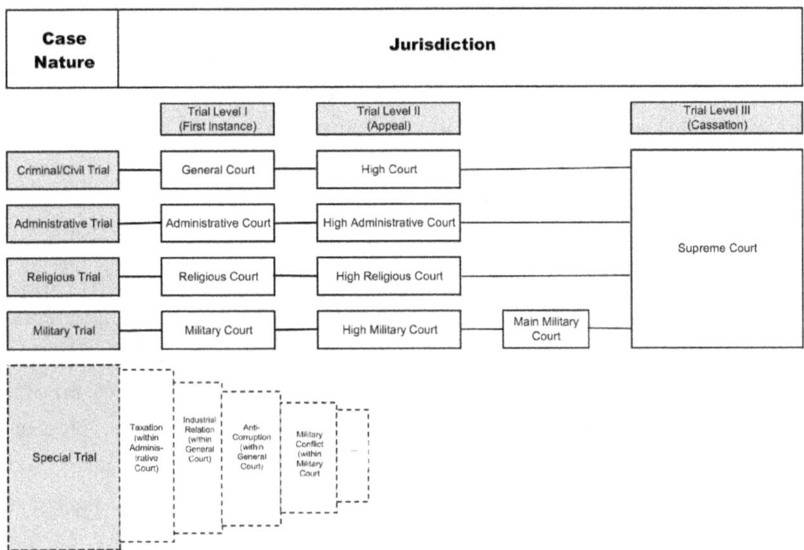

Figure 1 The structure of the Indonesian judicial system. This figure can also be found online at www.cambridge.org/muniroh.

shadaqah (ENG charitable giving), and sharia economics. These matters fall under the jurisdiction of religious courts by law for Muslim citizens, rather than by personal or administrative choice. Military courts are empowered to handle offenses committed by soldiers or individuals recognized as soldiers, as designated by the army commander and approved by the Minister of Justice and Human Rights. They also have jurisdiction over internal military disputes and civil cases connected to military offenses. The structure of the Indonesian judicial system is illustrated in Figure 1 (cf. Butt & Lindsey, 2018, p.84).

Within this court structure, there are typically two stages of appeal. The initial appeal is made to a higher court (High Court), and the second option is to file a cassation appeal to the Supreme Court, which is the highest court. In general, most cases are handled by a panel of three judges, with some exceptions (see Article 11 Section (1) Law 48 of 2009 on Judicial Power).

It is important to note that the Constitutional Court is not part of the organizational hierarchy of the regular court system in Indonesia. The Constitutional Court is an independent judicial body with nine judges, and it serves as the initial and ultimate authority for cases that fall under its jurisdiction. The Constitutional Court's recent work has included handling disputes on related to the results of the 2024 general election. Prior to that, the court also reviewed the legal requirements for presidential and vice-presidential candidates, which was an important and controversial process leading up to the 2024 election. The Constitutional Court is responsible for resolving matters related to the Constitution, such as interpreting its clauses and deciding whether laws and government activities comply with the Constitution. Acting independently from the usual court system, the Constitutional Court has a crucial role in maintaining the foundations of Indonesia's constitutional democracy. All decisions made by the Constitutional Court are final and binding.

The hierarchical structure of the court system in Indonesia is used for both civil and criminal law system to maintain order and resolve disputes within Indonesian society. The civil law system in Indonesia covers a range of non-criminal legal matters, which are primarily governed by the Indonesian Civil Code (Arifin, 2020). Examples of civil cases include contract disputes, property rights and ownership issues, family law matters (such as marriage, divorce, and inheritance), as well as commercial and business-related conflicts. In civil cases, the emphasis is on how individuals relate to one another and their respective rights and obligations. The plaintiff bears the responsibility of proving their claims. Civil courts have the authority to grant rulings for monetary compensation, specific fulfilment of obligations, or other fair solutions.

Indonesia's hierarchical court system, handling diverse civil and criminal cases, offers significant potential for forensic linguistic research. Article 195 of the Criminal Procedure Code and Article 13 of the Law on Judicial Power mandate public access to court proceedings, except in restricted cases (Amarini et al., 2023). Researchers may observe and collect data but must obtain prior permission from relevant authorities. Unlike the Constitutional Court, the High and Supreme Courts do not hold hearings but decide cases based on lower court records.

Despite its potential, research in courtroom interactions remains sparse. Linguistic researchers predominantly focus on interactions in general courts rather than specialized courts, and very few have examined appeals to higher courts or cassation appeals to the High Court from forensic linguistic perspectives.

The introduction of electronic court services which commenced in 2018 now allows registered users to manage their legal matters online. This comprehensive service includes features such as online case registration (e-Filing), online payment of court fees (e-Payment), electronic issuance of summonses (e-Summons), and conducting trials via online platforms (e-Litigation). These digital tools streamline the legal process, making it more accessible, efficient, and convenient for all parties involved (please visit e-Court *Mahkamah Agung,* ENG Supreme Court).

For forensic linguistic researchers, these digital innovations offer significant benefits. Researchers can now access court decisions more easily and check schedules for specific proceedings in the relevant courts, facilitating observation and data collection. This accessibility enhances the scope and efficiency of linguistic studies in the judicial context.

However, despite these advancements, substantive and technical challenges persist within the system (Amarini et al., 2023; Rossner et al., 2021; Tiwisia et al., 2023). The existing legal frameworks and regulations have yet to fully address the gaps needed to ensure that digital court processes are conducted with the same rigor and integrity as traditional proceedings. One significant concern is the reduced transparency of online proceedings, which may not align with the Indonesian Criminal Procedure Code's requirement for trials to be open to the public. Consequently, there is a pressing need to amend the Indonesian Criminal Procedure Code or introduce separate legislation to adequately regulate and support electronic court proceedings.

Meanwhile, criminal laws in Indonesia are substantively sourced from the *Kitab Undang-Undang Hukum Pidana* (KUHP) (ENG the Criminal Code) (Butt & Lindsey, 2020). The Indonesian Criminal Code is derived from the *Wetboek van Strafrecht voor Nederlands-Indië* (WvS-NI), which was imposed by the Dutch colonial government in 1918 (Butt, 2023; Faisal et al., 2024). This colonial-era legal framework has served as the foundation of Indonesia's criminal law system. Since 1963, efforts to codify genuine national values and shift away from the colonial paradigm of criminal law in Indonesia have been ongoing. These efforts culminated in December 2022 with the completion of the New Criminal Code, which accommodates Adat Criminal Law (see Butt, 2023; Yoserwan, 2024) and embodies a complex array of ideas aimed at achieving substantive justice (see Butt, 2023; Faisal et al., 2024).

The KUHP defines various criminal acts and the applicable penalties for those who commit them. The procedures for criminal cases are outlined in the *Kitab Undang-undang Hukum Acara Pidana*, or KUHAP (ENG the Code of Criminal Procedure), as per Law Number 8 of 1981. The KUHAP regulates the duties of the police and prosecutors, as well as the rules governing arrests, warrants, detention, searches, provision of legal aid, management of evidence, trial procedures, and the appeals process for most categories of criminal cases (Butt & Lindsey, 2020). The state prosecutes criminal cases, with public prosecutors serving as representatives. It is the prosecution's responsibility to prove the defendant's guilt beyond a reasonable doubt. Defendants, if found guilty, may be subject to penalties including fines, imprisonment, or, in certain instances, the death penalty. Further discussion about the procedural aspects of criminal law is provided in Section 1.4.2.

Due to historical factors, many terms in Indonesian civil and criminal law are derived from Dutch or Latin, rendering the legal language highly specialized.

While the language of the law is formally Indonesian and used uniformly across the country, some legal registers including numerous archaic and technical terms unfamiliar to most laypersons are still found. These legal terms underscore the distinct and technical nature of the Indonesian legal language, which remains largely confined to the professional sphere of lawyers, judges, and other legal practitioners, rather than being part of the everyday Indonesian lexicon. For example, words like *posita/positum* (ENG basis of the claim/grounds for the lawsuit), *petitum* (ENG the claims/demands in the lawsuit), *repliek* (ENG the plaintiff's rebuttal), *duplik* (ENG the defendant's response to the repliek), *verstek* (ENG a default judgment rendered in the absence of the defendant or without the defendant's presence), and *verzet* (ENG an objection or opposition to a *verstek* judgment) are deeply rooted in the country's colonial legal heritage, but are not widely used outside of legal contexts (Abubakar & Din, 2022).

Forensic linguistics can play a critical role in addressing these challenges. By analyzing and interpreting the specialized legal language, forensic linguists can contribute to the translation and simplification of legal documents (e.g. Marlia et al., 2023), making them more accessible to nonlegal professionals and the general public. This includes translating complex legal terms into plain language without compromising their legal accuracy, thereby bridging the gap between technical legal discourse and lay understanding.

Customary or *Adat* Law

Customary legal system or *adat* law is an ethnic legal tradition based on the long-standing and deeply ingrained values of the Indonesian people, as well as the community's own understanding of justice and peace (Lukito, 2012). As Indonesia is rich in diverse ethnicities (more than 600 ethnicities spread over some 17,000 islands), there is no single Indonesian customary law, but rather various regional customary laws, such as Adat law of Aceh, Java, Minangkabau, and so on (Mutaqin, 2011; Tamma & Duile, 2020). Therefore, Mutaqin (2011, p. 352) said that "no single scholar, even if he is an Indonesian, can be an expert of *adat* law."

A key feature of these customary laws is that it operates in the languages of the respective ethnic groups and have specific domain of application, which may differ from one region to another (Butt & Lindsey, 2018; Warman et al., 2018). The use of these languages is central to their transmission and practice, reflecting cultural values and ensuring the credibility of customary legal systems.

The *adat* law primarily governs matters related to land ownership and usage (e.g. Bakker, 2023; Fitzpatrick, 1999, 2007; Simarmata, 2019). Additionally, it encompasses certain aspects of family law, including regulations around marriage, divorce, and inheritance (e.g. Deliana & Rauf, 2022; Judiasih & Fakhriah, 2018; Thalib, 2023). Customary law also plays a role in the handling and resolution of a select number of civil and criminal disputes (see Law Number 30 of 1999 on Arbitration and Alternative Dispute Resolutions). In these cases, customary law often employs restorative approaches, which focus on repairing the harm caused and restoring harmony within the community, rather than solely on punitive measures (Budianto et al., 2022; Wardhani et al., 2022). Customary law is mainly practiced in rural and remote areas, where limited state presence leaves legal matters to local traditions.

However, as urbanization and economic development have continued to transform Indonesia since the 2010s, with the increasing numbers of people migrating to cities, the adherence and practice of customary law is steadily declining (Butt & Lindsey, 2018; Priambodo, 2018). This trend is driven by the growing influence of the national Indonesian language and the state's formal legal institutions in urban settings, which has led to the gradual erosion of the linguistic and cultural foundations of customary law. As a result, customary law's wider relevance and applicability have been increasingly undermined, especially among the populations that have relocated from rural areas to major cities. Nevertheless, customary law remains an important and influential legal tradition in many remote parts of Indonesia, where ethnic and indigenous communities continue to maintain strong connections to their ancestral lands and traditional governance structures (e.g. Salahuddin et al., 2023; Yulia et al., 2023).

Forensic linguistics can play a valuable role in the understanding, documentation, and application of *hukum adat* (customary laws) in Indonesia which is deeply rooted in oral traditions and expressed through diverse local languages. To date, there has been little to no forensic linguistic research focused on the intersection of language and customary law in Indonesia, making this a promising area for future exploration. Forensic linguists can contribute by documenting and analyzing oral testimonies, ceremonial language, and patterns of discourse used in traditional dispute resolution processes. They can also provide linguistic analysis of customary legal texts or oral statements. They can help clarify ambiguities and ensure that customary norms are correctly interpreted in formal legal settings. This is particularly valuable in a country where *adat* (ENG custom) often intersects with state and religious laws. Despite its importance, this area of research remains relatively underexplored, presenting opportunities for further scholarly and practical contributions.

Sharia Law

The other significant legal tradition applied in Indonesia is the religious legal system based on Islamic Sharia law. Indonesia, with over 80 percent of its population being Muslim, is considered one of the largest Muslim-majority countries in the world. However, it is important to note that Indonesia is not an Islamic state and does not apply Islamic law as the supreme source of law in the constitution and national legislation. Instead, the state ideology *Pancasila* (ENG the five pillars; Soekarno refers to it as *Weltanschauung* in German, roughly equivalent to the English word "worldview") serves as the foundational principle.

Only the province of Aceh in Indonesia currently enforces Sharia law. The application of Islamic law in Aceh is provided under Law Number 44 of 1999, which grants the province a special autonomous status, as well as *Keputusan Presiden* (ENG Presidential Decree) Number 11 of 2003. Unlike customary law, which is primarily unwritten, the implementation of Sharia law in Aceh is codified in the form of Aceh Qanun, or local regulations, for example, Aceh Qanun Number 6 of 2014 about *Qanun Jinayat* (ENG Aceh Criminal Code) and Aceh Qanun Number 7 of 2013 about *Hukum Acara Jinayat* (ENG *Aceh Criminal Procedure Code*). These codes operate alongside the national Indonesian Criminal Code and Indonesian Criminal Procedure Code in Aceh, reflecting the province's special autonomous status and the application of Islamic criminal law within the broader Indonesian legal framework. The ulama council, also known in Indonesian as the *Majelis Permusyawaratan Ulama*, has been a key institution in the enforcement of this Qanun. Additionally, *Wilayatul Hisbah* (ENG the Sharia police) has also its relevance. Furthermore, *Mahkamah Syariah* (ENG the Islamic courts) have played a significant role in legal operation (Cammack & Feener, 2012).

Unlike customary law, which operates primarily in local languages, the Aceh Qanun is predominantly written in Indonesian, incorporating specific terminologies derived from Arabic. Terms such as *jarīmah, uqūbat, hudūd, tazīr, khalwat, ikhtilāth, liwāth, musāhaqah,* and *khamar* have been integrated into *Kamus Besar Bahasa Indonesia* (ENG the Great Indonesian Language Dictionary). However, their enforcement can sometimes pose challenges due to linguistic and cultural differences (Abubakar & Din, 2022).

The coexistence of Sharia law, as codified in the Aceh Qanun, alongside the national legal system and customary law in Indonesia reflects the country's rich religious and cultural diversity. This pluralistic legal landscape continues to be a subject of ongoing discussion and negotiation within the Indonesian context.

Forensic linguistics can enhance fairness, transparency, and communication in Sharia-based legal processes by analyzing texts, judgments, and testimonies to identify inconsistencies, clarify interpretations, and ensure equitable application of legal language. Examining how key terms are understood across cases supports consistency and fairness. Although this area remains underexplored, a notable study by Yusuf, Mansur, and Muthalib (2024) applies legal linguistics and critical discourse analysis to public opinion on Qanun Putroe Phang, an Aceh regulation on governance and women's and children's rights. The authors recommend revising the qanun toward a persuasive rather than mandatory approach, aligning with Acehnese values and social dynamics. This emerging research highlights the potential of language–law studies to inform Sharia-based legal practices while respecting cultural and religious contexts.

1.3.2 Indonesian Criminal Law and Procedures

This section focuses on the procedural elements of criminal law. The elements, such as regulations concerning police investigations, prosecutions, and trials, are outlined in the *Kitab Undang-Undang Hukum Acara Pidana* or KUHAP (ENG Criminal Procedure Code). In contrast to the Criminal Code, which was initially enacted in 1918, KUHAP is not a product of colonialism. Instead, it was created as the Indonesian government efforts to replace the Dutch procedural code, which had been in force since 1926, and address modern demands for the management of criminal justice. KUHAP is not impacted by the New Criminal Code (Butt, 2023).

KUHAP outlines four stages of criminal procedure (Butt & Lindsey, 2020). The first is the *penyelidikan* (ENG preliminary investigation), aimed at determining whether a crime has occurred. The second is *penyidikan* (ENG the main investigation) which seeks to gather further information and evidence, and identify suspects. At this stage, *praperadilan* (ENG pre-trial hearings) may also occur. The third stage is *penuntutan* (ENG prosecution*)*, during which prosecutors prepare their case against the accused for presentation in court. Lastly, *pengadilan* (ENG the trial) takes place, where a panel of typically three judges reviews the case, determines the defendant's guilt or innocence, and, if found guilty, assigns punishment. This section does not detail further about KUHAP (for further readings, see Butt & Lindsey, 2020). Instead, it will link these stages to the potential importance of forensic linguistics thus far.

Among the four stages, the first and second stages often attract public concern, particularly because the police, who lead the investigation process, have been repeatedly reported for employing coercive practices against suspects during custody and interrogation, according to *Komnas HAM* (ENG the

National Human Rights Commission) (Pratama & Ibrahim, 2024) and the Institute for Criminal Justice Reform (Azeez, 2024). Although the Indonesian police have regulations grounded in principles of human rights and ethics, they often struggle to implement these principles in practice (Muniroh & Heydon, 2022).

To address these issues, initiatives have been launched, including training programs aimed at transforming traditional interrogation methods into investigative interviewing practices (Asplund, 2019). *Kompolnas RI* (ENG Indonesia's National Police Commission), a supervisory body established to promote police accountability, advocates for the nationwide adoption of investigative interviewing techniques and the use of designated interview rooms (Hatoum, 2023).

In this context, forensic linguistics plays a crucial role in enhancing police investigators' awareness of how language can influence or minimize the potential for torture. It also facilitates research on the discourse used in police interviews, including language employed by investigators, witnesses, victims, and suspects. This area of investigation has been explored by Indonesian scholars, as will be detailed in Section 3.

As noted by Muniroh (2019) and Muniroh and Aziz (2016), recording is not mandatory during police interviews in Indonesia. Consequently, linguists interested in police investigations may encounter challenges in collecting natural data (see Muniroh & Heydon, 2024). In contrast to police interviewing, which lacks transparency, the openness of court proceedings to the public, as discussed previously, presents a more promising area for investigation.

1.3.3 Sociocultural Contexts

In addition to the legal system and criminal law shaping the development of forensic linguistics in Indonesia, sociocultural contexts also play a significant role in influencing its progress. These sociocultural factors encompass Indonesia's linguistic diversity, the wide range of ethnic groups and religions, the unique sociocultural norms that define interactions and communication within the country, and literacy of Indonesian people. Together, these elements create both challenges and opportunities for the application of forensic linguistics in addressing legal issues.

Linguistic Diversity

Indonesia possesses an exceptional richness in linguistic diversity. Zein (2020) observed and support Steinhauer's assertion (Steinhauer, 1994) that although the exact number of languages spoken globally is unknown, it is estimated that

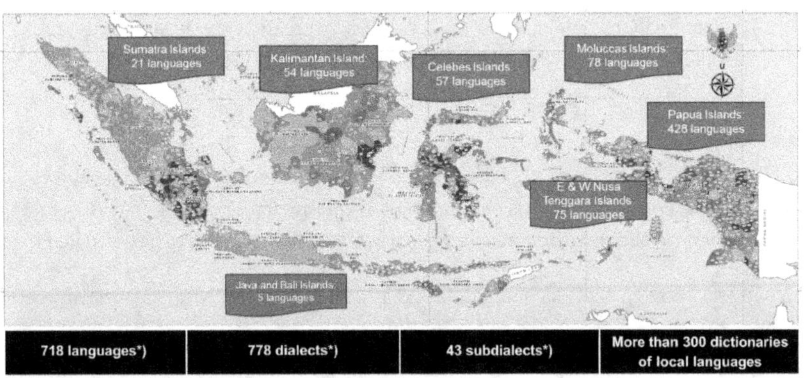

Figure 2 Language maps of Indonesia (Aziz, 2024). This figure can also be found online at www.cambridge.org/muniroh.

one-tenth of them are spoken in Indonesia. This claim is later reinforced by Florey and Himmelmann (2010, p. 123), who state that Indonesia represents 10.7 percent of the world's languages. At the current statistics as shown in Figure 2, there are 718 languages,[3] 778 dialects,[4] and 43 subdialects[5] collected from 2,560 observation areas throughout Indonesia under the Local Language Mapping Projects, 2009-2019 (Aziz, 2024).

With Indonesia's rich diversity of languages, cultures, and ethnicities, law enforcement and the delivery of justice face both significant opportunities and challenges. Linguistic differences can complicate communication within legal settings, particularly during police investigations and court proceedings. While Indonesian is mandated as the language of the courtroom and judicial proceedings (Article 53 of the Indonesian Criminal Code), the reality of multilingual interactions necessitates careful management of language issues.

Indonesian regulations have long acknowledged the importance of language in legal contexts. Law Number 8 of 1981 on Criminal Procedure explicitly references the role of interpreters in Articles 53 Section (1) and Article 177 Section (1), as follows:

---

[3] We call it a language when it is regarded and widely used as a standard form by its speakers. This form is also taught formally at schools and used in formal situations.

[4] The term *dialect* is used to refer to the varieties in the language found across different geographical distributions, i.e. geographical dialect. For example, Javanese is a language spoken mainly in the regions of Central Java, East Java, Jogjakarta provinces, although the language is also spoken in some other parts of Indonesia.

[5] Subdialect is a further subdivision within a dialect. Osing, a variety found in Banyuwangi Regency of East Java province is classified as a subdialect of East Java dialect.

Article 53 Section (1)
In examinations conducted at the level of investigation and trial, the suspect
or defendant has the right to receive the assistance of an interpreter at any
time, as referred to in Article 177.

Article 177 Section (1)
If the defendant or witness does not understand the Indonesian language, the
presiding judge of the trial shall appoint an interpreter who has sworn an oath
or made a pledge to accurately translate everything that needs to be translated.

However, the regulations lack detailed provisions regarding the qualifications
required for interpreters in legal settings. This gap is further exacerbated by certain
attitudes among law enforcement officers regarding language use. Overconfidence
in their own linguistic abilities or assumptions about language familiarity can
lead officers to forego engaging professional interpreters. In some cases, court
staff members, such as judicial case analysts, archivists, or even security personnel, are appointed as interpreters solely based on their language background,
regardless of their professional training or expertise in legal interpretation (see
e.g. Tampubolon, 2024). For instance, letters issued by the court (see: Supreme
Court of Indonesia Legal Products,[6] accessed December 10, 2024) stated that
assigned staff members were considered competent and capable of serving as
interpreters in courtroom proceedings. The letters also outlined the responsibilities
of courtroom interpreters: (1) render the language accurately and completely, (2)
remain impartial and avoid taking sides, and (3) prevent conflicts of interest.

Addressing these issues requires establishing clear interpreter qualifications
and standards in legal settings to ensure fairness and accuracy in multilingual
courtrooms. This highlights the importance of professionalizing the role of
interpreters to safeguard justice and equity within Indonesia's pluralistic legal
landscape.

Another issue related to linguistic diversity is the differences in people's
perceptions or attitudes toward particular languages, dialects, or vernacular
languages. These views can often lead to conflicts in cross-linguistic interactions, especially when some are viewed as more prestigious than others. In
Indonesia, such interactions are particularly common due to migration from one
region to another for work or educational purposes, which brings together
speakers of different languages. For example, the distinction between standard
Bahasa Indonesia (a high variety) and the vernacular Bahasa Indonesia of

---

[6] Tenggarong, East Kalimantan https://jdih.mahkamahagung.go.id/index.php/legal-product/penun
jukan-penerjemah-dalam-persidangan-pengadilan-negeri-tenggarong-kelas-ib-1/detail;
Banyuwangi, East Java, https://jdih.mahkamahagung.go.id/index.php/legal-product/penunjukan-
penerjemah-dalam-persidangan-pada-pengadilan-negeri-banyuwangi/detail, accessed December
18, 2024.

Eastern Indonesia (a low variety) illustrates this dynamic. The unique dialectal characteristics of Eastern Indonesian languages – phonological, lexical, and morphological – can raise issues of linguistic racism and privilege (Wijaya & Rizal, 2023). These variations in Bahasa Indonesia often lead to further forensic linguistic issues, such as bullying and hate speech.

Another relevant illustration to issues related to linguistic diversity is the disputed meanings of words stemming from conflicting prescriptive and descriptive views on the emerging use of language, such as slang. A notable case involves the word *"anjay."*[7] According to Indonesian YouTuber Lutfi Agizal, this word should be prohibited to use as it can damage the morality of Indonesian youth, and those who use it should be punished for its insulting nature. As a response to this, the National Commission for Child Protection released a statement purporting to ban the word, arguing that it diminishes someone's honor and dignity, which can be punishable by law under verbal violence (Utami, 2020). This statement received strong reactions from Indonesian netizens. In this context, both the YouTuber and the National Commission viewed the word prescriptively, while linguists approached it descriptively, recognizing that the meaning of the word may vary depending on the context of its use.

Ethnicity and Religion

According to the 2020 Population Census by BPS Statistics Indonesia, Indonesia has a population of 278.7 million and over 600 ethnic groups (Zein, 2020). The five largest groups are the Javanese (40.2% of the population), Sundanese (15.5%), Batak (3.6%), Sulawesi (3.22%), and Madurese (3.03%) (Na'im & Syaputra, 2011). Most Indonesians identify as Muslims (87.18%), followed by Christians (6.96%), Catholics (2.91%), Hindus (1.69%), Buddhists (0.72%), Confucians (0.05%), and adherents of other religions (0.5%).

As a multi-ethnic and multi-religious nation, Indonesia generally maintains peaceful interethnic and interreligious relationships. Core values like tolerance and Bhinneka Tunggal Ika (Unity in Diversity) foster harmony, while Pancasila, the state ideology, promotes mutual respect and cooperation. Together, these principles serve as social capital for violence prevention and conflict resolution (Hartoyo et al., 2020).

However, interethnic and interreligious conflicts have occurred, particularly after the fall of the New Order regime in 1998 (Dewantara et al., 2024; Liu &

---

[7] The word *"anjay"* is a colloquial variant of *"anjing"* (ENG dog), similar to terms like *"anjrit,"* *"njiir,"* *"anjir,"* and *"anjas."* It can serve as a word to express strong emotions, such as surprise or amazement or a curse word or offensive language used to insult. The meaning might vary depending on situational contexts of its use.

Ricks, 2022). Key causes include economic inequality, lack of understanding of religious differences, and perceptions of unfair treatment (Rasyid et al., 2023). Challenges persist, including tensions involving the Chinese community – Indonesia's fifteenth largest ethnic group (Adi & Bahri, 2023; Sinaga et al., 2024) – as well as issues related to Islamic radicalism and terrorism.

An example of interethnic conflicts can be illustrated by the tendencies of certain ethnic groups, such as the Batak, who are known for speaking directly and with a high tone. This directness can lead to perceptions of anger or aggression. In contrast, other ethnicities, such as the Javanese or Sundanese, often communicate in a more indirect and soft-spoken manner. These differing communication styles can create misunderstandings and tensions between groups, highlighting the impact of cultural differences on interpersonal interactions. Another illustration can be found in Dewantara et al.'s research on verbal violence and discrimination in Multi-Ethnic Schools in West Kalimantan, Indonesia (Dewantara et al., 2024).

In Indonesia, sensitive issues related to ethnicity and religion are categorized under SARA (*Suku, Agama, Ras, dan Antargolongan* – ENG Ethnicity, Religion, Race, and Intergroup Relations). These aspects are central to defining verbal violence such as hate speech and understanding social tensions. Addressing SARA-related challenges is essential for promoting tolerance and unity in Indonesia's multicultural society.

Forensic linguistics has played a significant role in addressing SARA-related conflicts. By analyzing the language used in media, legal documents, and public discourse, forensic linguists can identify hate speech, inflammatory rhetoric, or biased narratives that exacerbate tensions. They can contribute to developing clearer guidelines for detecting and prosecuting hate speech under Indonesian law, ensuring that SARA-related violations are addressed effectively (see Section 4).

Sociocultural Norms

In Indonesia, a remarkably diverse nation, linguistic and cultural variations naturally emerge across its many ethnic groups. Despite this diversity, Indonesian society has traditionally emphasized unity, harmony, and collective responsibility, as reflected in the national ethos of gotong royong – mutual cooperation and the prioritization of shared goals (Butt, 2023; Rahardjo, 1994). These values live in community-based interactions which are hold in face-to-face communication mode. However, this landscape has been shifting since 2015, driven by modernization, globalization, and democratization (Abdullah et al., 2019). Increasingly, individual interests are prioritized over collective values. In the past, Indonesian collectivism was the norm, with the concept of *aku* (ENG I, the self) illustrating that individual identity was deeply embedded in community relationships. This sharply contrasted with Western individualism, where the self is perceived as autonomous and independent (Rahardjo, 1994).

Today, with the rise of "selfism" or individualism, Indonesians are becoming more assertive and self-focused, more aware of honor and reputation in social interactions, particularly in urban and digital communication. What was once perceived as confrontational or disruptive to communal harmony is now becoming more commonplace. This cultural shift has led to social fragmentation and a weakening of traditional ethical frameworks, contributing to increased social tensions. Conflicts related to privacy, self-image, and individual rights have become more apparent.

The adverse effects of technology have drastically changed the way people interact and communicate, leading to a significant sociocultural shift. It has created new realities in which individuals navigate both a digital world and the physical one. Unlike face-to-face communication, digital communication allows for interaction without the limitations of time and geography, enabling exchanges that are often instant and capable of reaching a global audience. While individuals enjoy a degree of freedom in presenting themselves and sharing their interests – thanks to the possibility of anonymity – they may not realize that their messages or posts in the digital realm can leave a lasting trace. This permanence can have unintended consequences, impacting their reputation and privacy in ways they might not anticipate.

Digital communication has also given rise to a new genre of language practices, blending spoken language styles with written forms. Therefore, digital literacy is essential, as many Indonesians may lack this skill, resulting in problematic language use in the virtual world, including hoaxes, hate speech, slander, fraud, manipulation, insults, defamation, plagiarism, and more (Saifullah, 2021).

This transformation underscores the growing importance of forensic linguistics in addressing expressions that may lead to hate speech, insults, or defamation not only in face-to-face communication but also in digital world. As communication norms evolve, forensic linguistics plays a critical role in providing expert testimony and analysis to navigate disputes and uphold justice in a changing societal landscape.

2 Historical Development of Forensic Linguistics in Indonesia

2.1 Origins, Early Influences, and Key Milestones

Indonesian history reveals that cases involving language, which could result in imprisonment or other punishments, have occurred since the Soekarno era or Old Order (1945–1966), continued through the Suharto era or New Order (1966–1998) administration, and persist to this day. During the Old and New Order periods, the term "forensic linguistics" was not yet in use, language-related cases were rarely brought to court, and the analysis of language in connection with crimes was referred to simply as common language analysis. Criticism directed at the government or authorities during these periods often led to punishment to the critics, which could be in the form of imprisonment. This is in line with what Human Rights Watch (2010, p. 2) reported:

> Holding public demonstrations protesting corruption, writing letters to the editor, complaining about fraud, registering formal complaints about acts of impropriety by politicians, and writing and publishing news reports about sensitive subjects are common practices in a democratic society. But in Indonesia, such criticism can lead to criminal charges and land you in prison, even if what you say is true.

According to the literature, early language-related cases frequently involved critics and defamation, with many of these cases pitting citizens against government or journalists against authorities (Margiyono, 2010; Teguh, 2019). One notable example is Mochtar Lubis, the editor-in-chief of the newspaper *Indonesia Raya*, who was imprisoned during the 1950s. He served a ten-year sentence after being accused of criticizing and defaming the government during the Old Order under President Soekarno. Following his release, during the Soeharto era, Lubis continued his critical reporting through Indonesia Raya, publishing exposés on corruption within Pertamina, Indonesia's state oil company. As a result, he was imprisoned again for two and a half months, and his newspaper was banned (Teguh, 2019).

Another example is Ashadi Siregar. In 1973, he was brought to trial for publishing an article titled "*Mukaddimah*" in *Sandi* magazine. The article reportedly contained sharp criticisms of government policies and highlighted the societal impact of authoritarianism, making it a target in a political climate intolerant of dissent. Ashadi was sentenced to one year in prison, and *Sandi* magazine was subsequently banned from publication (Badan Pengembangan dan Pembinaan Bahasa, 2016). Two other cases worth mentioning here, namely the imprisonment to Sri Bintang Pamungkas for his affront expressions (defamation) addressed to President Soeharto. The other one was the use of linguistic expressions *Ada Tomy di Tenabang* (ENG There is Tomy in Tanah Abang – a district in Jakarta) on the cover of the March 2003 edition of Tempo magazine. This phrase referred to prominent Indonesian businessman Tomy Winata. Winata took offense to the reporting, deeming it inaccurate and defamatory. Tempo had suggested his involvement in the Tanah Abang Market fire incident and alleged he secured a 53 billion IDR renovation project for the market. This resulted in the charges to the editors and the magazine was then banned.

During that era, Indonesia already had legal provisions for defamation inherited from the *Herzien Inlandsch Reglement* (HIR) of the Dutch colonial period, which were codified in the Indonesian Criminal Code (KUHP) under Chapter XVI, Articles 310–321. These articles provided the legal framework frequently used to prosecute defamation cases. Below are the relevant provisions from Articles 310 and 311, which were commonly invoked:

Article 310

(1) The person who intentionally harms someone's honor or reputation by charging him with a certain fact, with the obvious intent to give publicity thereof, shall, being guilty of slander, be punished by a maximum imprisonment of nine months or a maximum fine of three hundred rupiahs

(2) If this takes place by means of writings or portraits disseminated, openly demonstrated or put up, the principal shall, being guilty of libel, be punished with a maximum imprisonment of one year and four months or a maximum fine of three hundred rupiahs

(3) Neither slander nor libel shall exist as far as the principal obviously has acted in the general interest or for a necessary defense.

Article 311

(1) Any person who commits the crime of slander or libel in ease proof of truth of the charged fact is permitted, shall, if he does not produce said proof and the charge has been made against his better judgment, being guilty of calumny, be punished by a maximum imprisonment of four years.

(2) Deprivation of rights mentioned in Article 35 first to thirdly may be pronounced.

However, this defamation law has raised significant concerns among scholars and human rights activists due to its negative impact in Indonesia. It is frequently used as a tool of official repression to criminalize individuals and restrict freedom of expression – a right explicitly protected by Indonesia's Constitution (Heryanto, 1995; Human Rights Watch, 2010). Article 28 Section (e) states, "Every person shall have the right to the freedom of association and expression of opinion," while Article 28 Section (f) affirms, "Every person shall have the right to communicate and obtain information for the development of his/her personal life and social environment, and shall have the right to seek, acquire, possess, keep, process, and convey information using all available channels."

During the Old Order, the involvement of language experts in legal proceedings was almost nonexistent. This absence can be attributed to the prevailing perception that legal matters primarily required expertise in fields such as law, politics, sociology, human rights, communication, or journalism (Heryanto, 1995; Margiyono, 2010). Language analysis, particularly in legal contexts, was not yet regarded as a significant or relevant tool for resolving disputes or clarifying evidence in court.

This trend continued into the New Order, as demonstrated by the courts' rejection of language experts as witnesses in 1989, even when requested by defendants and their lawyers (Heryanto, 1995). This decision highlighted the limited recognition of their potential contributions to legal proceedings at the time. Furthermore, linguistic scholarship during this period primarily focused on theoretical pursuits, such as the study of suffixes, complex sentences, and grammatical structures, rather than practical applications like forensic linguistics. Additionally, linguistic studies were more oriented toward corpus development, language standardization, and language learning, with little emphasis on applied research, let alone forensic purposes. Heryanto (1995) indicates that the first recorded instance of a language expert being invited to court by prosecutors occurred on August 8, 1995, when Drs. Lukman Hakim provided testimony in the Permadi insult case at the Sleman District Court.

The rejection of language experts by the courts was largely influenced by the shortcomings in the regulation and provision of expert testimonies in Indonesia. Law Number 8 of 1981 on the Indonesian Criminal Procedure Code (KUHAP) does not clearly or comprehensively define expert testimony or specify the qualifications required to be considered an expert. This lack of clarity in the legal framework contributed to the courts' limited acceptance of expert witnesses, including language experts. Expert testimony, recognized as valid evidence under the law, is addressed in only one article. Found in Part Four, Chapter X, Article 186 of the Criminal Procedure Code states: "Expert testimony is what an expert declares in court." Similarly, the norms governing the qualifications of an expert are minimal. Article 1 Section (28) of the Criminal Procedure Code merely defines expert testimony as "the testimony provided by a person with specific expertise on matters required to clarify a criminal case for the purposes of an investigation" (Raspati, 2012). However, this Article does not clarify whether an expert's explanation can be submitted as written statement alone or if the expert must appear in court to present and defend their statement (Butt & Nathaniel, 2024).

This illustration clearly highlights that in Indonesia, the primary focus of language in legal contexts has been its use as evidence. However, this does not imply that other areas, such as spoken language in legal processes and written language in legal documents, are without issues. For instance, violations of human rights during investigative processes at police stations and the ambiguity of legal texts remain a significant concern – one that forensic linguistics can help address. This raises a critical question: when did people begin recognizing or referring to the practice of providing expert testimonies in legal cases as forensic linguistics?

The emergence of forensic linguistics in Indonesia can be categorized into three key factors. First, the influence of Indonesian scholars who studied abroad either through degree programs or specialized courses, and returned to disseminate their knowledge. Second, the growing number of Indonesian scholars exposed to forensic linguistic research, literature, and publications, which helped to expand awareness and understanding of the field. Third, the increasing recognition of language's pivotal role in the legal and judicial system, particularly following the enactment of the Electronic Information and Transactions Law in 2008 (Law Number 11 of 2008) and its amendment in 2016 (Law Number 19 of 2016).

The authors of this Element are included in the first category. More particularly, E. Aminudin Aziz played a pivotal role as one of the pioneering Indonesian scholars in the early dissemination of forensic linguistics in the country (see Aziz, 2012, 2016; Mira, 2002; Rustandi, 2011). His journey in forensic linguistics began while pursuing his doctoral degree in linguistics at Monash University Australia in 1997. To our knowledge, exposure to forensic linguistics among Indonesian scholars during this period was still rare, and even fewer pursued MA or doctoral studies specifically in this field.

During this time, he received formal training in forensic linguistics and was involved in assisting with language analyses for forensic cases involving local languages in Australia. He was also introduced to the work of Diana Eades on Aboriginal language cases during a Master class taught by Anne Pauwels. Yet, his theses fell under the area of Pragmatics, focusing on politeness phenomena in speech acts of refusals.

After completing his PhD in 2000, he returned to Indonesia and began teaching undergraduate sociolinguistics courses in the English language education program at Universitas Pendidikan Indonesia or UPI (ENG Indonesia University of Education), where R. Dian Dia-an Muniroh was one of his students. In these classes, he introduced forensic linguistics, incorporating it into the syllabus. The course included student presentations based on critical readings of sociolinguistic materials assigned from the first meeting. Muniroh had the opportunity to present and share her understanding of language and the law in Australia, focusing on the Kevin Condren case, in which Diana Eades served as an expert witness. This presentation marked Muniroh's introduction to forensic linguistics and sparked her interest in the field.

In October 2002, Aziz was interviewed by an Isola Pos[8] journalist and his explanation about forensic linguistics was published in this newspaper with the title "*Seorang Ahli Linguistik Bisa Memperingan Kerja Hakim*" (ENG A Linguistics Expert Can Ease a Judge's Work; see Figure 3) (Mira, 2002). This marked the first time the term "forensic linguistics" was used and disseminated through the media in Indonesia.

Another significant milestone in the dissemination and development of forensic linguistics in Indonesia was the international conference organized through a collaboration between the Universitas Pendidikan Indonesia (UPI) branch of the Linguistic Society of Indonesia, led by Aziz, and the Linguistic Society of Indonesia (https://www.mlindonesia.org/).[9] This event, known as *Kongres International Masyarakat Linguistik Indonesia* or KIMLI (ENG International Conference of the Linguistic Society of Indonesia), took place in Bandung, West Java, on October 9–12, 2011. Under the theme "Language and Nation Character Building," forensic linguistics was one of the main topics offered during the One Day Master Class offered in pre-conference session, alongside two other key areas discussed by linguists (Rustandi, 2011). The other two topics included Field Linguistics, which focused on mapping endangered languages, and Applied Linguistics, which explored models of English language teaching that emphasized critical thinking. The Master Class on forensic linguistics was well-attended by Indonesian scholars, journalists, and law enforcement officers. The conference featured Dr. Georgina Heydon, a forensic linguist from RMIT University in Melbourne, Australia, who delivered the Master Class and served as a keynote speaker. Her paper presented at KIMLI 2011, titled "Forensic Linguistics: Forms and Processes," was later published in the *Linguistik Indonesia* journal February 2014 (Heydon, 2014). This publication marked the first academic article on forensic linguistics to appear in an Indonesian journal.

---

[8] Isola Pos (commonly known as Isola) is a student newspaper published by the Student Press Unit of Universitas Pendidikan Indonesia (UPM UPI). The first edition (Introduction Edition) of Isola Pos was published in August 1991 using the offset printing system.

[9] www.inilah.com/upi-bandung-kembangkan-bidang-forensik-linguistik, accessed December 25, 2024.

Figure 3 The first campus newspaper publication on forensic linguistics.

Following this conference, Indonesian scholars reached a significant milestone by presenting their papers on forensic linguistics at the First Asia Regional Conference of the International Association of Forensic Linguists, held during July 5–7, 2012, in Kuala Lumpur, Malaysia. Under the theme "Forensic Linguistics/Language and Law: Researching Interdisciplinary Dimensions and Perspectives," Muniroh and Aziz, lecturers from Universitas Pendidikan Indonesia (UPI), presented a paper on the language used by defendants in corruption cases during courtroom proceedings. Another Indonesian presenter,

Susanto, a doctoral student in linguistics and phonetics at the English and Foreign Languages University in Hyderabad, India, delivered a paper on the use of an Indonesian speaker verification system to analyze authorship in corruption cases. Prior to the conference, Muniroh and Aziz participated in the 12th International Summer School in Forensic Linguistic Analysis (ISSFLA), an intensive training program facilitated by Professor Emeritus Malcolm Coulthard and Dr. Krzysztof Kredens of Aston University, United Kingdom. This program was held in conjunction with the conference and provided foundational knowledge and practical expertise in forensic linguistics. The ISSFLA equipped the authors with valuable insights and inspiration, sparking ideas for advancing forensic linguistics in Indonesia.

Another significant contribution to the development of forensic linguistics in Indonesia is the publication of two volumes of forensic linguistics textbooks by the Center for National Resilience Studies at Universitas Andalas, Padang, authored by Sawirman and his colleagues in 2014 and 2015, respectively. The first volume introduces readers to the fundamental concepts of forensic linguistics, including investigative logic, case exploration, and related concepts, supported by practical examples (Sawirman et al., 2014). The second volume provides detailed explanations of methods, as well as software and hardware tools, that can facilitate forensic linguistic analysis (Sawirman et al., 2015). In addition, *Badan Bahasa* (ENG the Agency for Language Development and Cultivation)[10] published the Guidelines for Forensic Linguistic Studies (Khatimah & Kusumawardani, 2016). This highlights the increasing exposure of Indonesian scholars to forensic linguistics through research, literature, and publications, which has significantly contributed to raising awareness and deepening understanding of the discipline.

Still within the realm of language as evidence, a significant milestone in the development of forensic linguistics in Indonesia is the enactment of the Electronic Information and Transactions Law (ITE Law) under Law No. 11 of 2008, and its subsequent amendment in 2016 (Law No. 19 of 2016). This legislation was designed to safeguard individual rights in online interactions, electronic transactions, intellectual property, and various business or consumer-related matters. Under the law, individuals who use social media platforms, Internet news portals, or television to intimidate or defame others can be charged with criminal offenses for insulting someone's dignity (see Article 27). Human rights activists, the media, and many members of the public believe

---

[10] *Badan Bahasa* (ENG The Agency for Language Development and Cultivation) is an official governmental institution in Indonesia operating under the Ministry of Education, Culture, Research, and Technology. The agency is dedicated to fostering the development, preservation, and promotion of the Indonesian language and other local languages across the archipelago.

this undermines free expression in Indonesia and tarnishes the nation's otherwise successful transition from an authoritarian regime to Southeast Asia's most robust democracy.

Since its introduction, the ITE Law has contributed to a steady rise in language-related cases in Indonesia's cyber domain, including defamation, hate speech, insults, and blasphemy. Between 2009 and 2014, the law led to the prosecution of seventy-one individuals in defamation cases (Zifana et al., 2021). One of the most notable cases, and the first known victim of the ITE Law, occurred in 2009 when Prita Mulyasari was detained for cyberdefamation. This followed the circulation of her email criticizing the treatment she received at a private hospital near Jakarta, which was shared in an online chat group (Batubara, 2009; LBH Masyarakat, 2009). According to 2020 data from the Supreme Court of the Republic of Indonesia on violations of the ITE Law, there were 193 recorded court decisions. Of these, 33 percent pertained to defamation, 21 percent to hate speech, 18 percent to violations of Article 27 paragraph 1 regarding criminal acts of indecency, and the remainder involved offenses such as unauthorized access, threats, forgery, and extortion (Pastika et al., 2023).

The increase in such cases is undeniably linked to the low digital literacy skills in Indonesia, a nation strongly influenced by oral traditions. These traditions, reflected in folklore and social interaction patterns, have shaped how Indonesian society engages with social media. As the role of language experts has gained recognition and linguistic analysis has become pivotal in the legal and judicial system, the demand for expertise in language-based cases has also risen. This trend aligns with the significant growth in the use of expert evidence in general in Indonesia over the past two decades (Butt & Nathaniel, 2024). Consequently, scholars are increasingly being invited to provide expert testimonies in court. These experts are mostly language lecturers from universities or *widyabasa* (ENG language specialists) from *Badan Bahasa*.

Building on the discussion of the involvement of language experts and the use of language as legal evidence, another critical area contributing to the development of forensic linguistics in Indonesia is scholars' focus on language use in legal processes, particularly in police interviews and legal interpreting. In such processes, instances of injustice in Indonesia have often stemmed from inadequate police interviewing practices (Meliala, 2001; Muniroh & Heydon, 2022). While the role of language experts in providing courtroom testimonies has been more widely recognized, scholarly involvement in analyzing language used in police interviews primarily began through research initiatives. For example, the establishment of the Forensic Linguistics Research Group at Universitas Pendidikan Indonesia in 2013, inspired by materials from

ISSFLA, marked a significant step. Aziz, Muniroh, and their team, supported by a research grant from the university, investigated the accuracy of police investigation reports. Their findings revealed that these police reports often failed to include all the information provided by interviewees during investigations (Aziz et al., 2013). The results of this research were shared in two key academic forums: a paper titled "Investigators' Questioning Strategies and Its Implications to Truth Disclosure" was presented at the KIMLI held on February 19–22, 2014, at the Sheraton Hotel in Bandar Lampung, and another paper titled "The Quality of Investigators' Questions in Police Investigation Reports" was presented at the 12th Biennial Conference of the International Association of Forensic Linguists (IAFL) at Guangdong University of Foreign Studies in Guangzhou, China, on July 6–9, 2015. Subsequent developments in this field include several early significant publications: a book chapter on contemporary police interviewing practices in Indonesia (Muniroh & Aziz, 2016), research on adapting cognitive interviewing techniques to Indonesian policing contexts (Muniroh, 2019), and a study on question types in police investigations involving children's cases (Bachari et al., 2019).

Legal interpreting, particularly court interpreting, is commonly required in criminal cases involving foreigners who do not speak Indonesian.[11] These foreigners may be expatriates, visitors, or tourists (Tampubolon, 2024). Notably, one of the pioneers of court interpreting in Indonesia is I Wayan Ana from Bali, who has been involved in this field since 1987 (Koagouw, 2022). Bali, being a major international tourist destination, has the highest demand for legal interpreters in the country (Ana, 2018). However, the field of legal interpreting faces significant challenges, including a shortage of qualified human resources and an imbalance between supply and demand.[12] Another area in forensic linguistics that draws the attention of Indonesian scholars, in addition to language as evidence and language in legal processes, is the study of legal language, particularly the textual analysis of legal documents. Notable publications in this area include the research report reconstructing legal language of the civil servant oath text (Aziz & Lukmana, 2013), investigations into legal language in regulations (Rifai, 2020; Shidarta, 2017), the characteristics of Indonesian legal language in notarial documents (Ana, 2020), and studies on translating legal texts (Amani et al., 2023; Sofyan & Rosa, 2021; Suryasa et al.,

---

[11] Court interpreting practices, see www.detik.com/bali/berita/d-6105042/suka-duka-wayan-ana-35-tahun-jadi-penerjemah-wna-di-pengadilan, https://www.bpk.go.id/assets/files/magazine/edisi-10-volii-oktober-2012_hal_60____80_.pdf, accessed December 29, 2024.

[12] Pre-service university students act as interpreters of Sasak language in the courtroom; see https://pa-selong.go.id/index.php/berita-seputar-peradilan/439-perkara-waris-mendominasi-kesehatian-di-pengadilan-agama-selong, accessed December 29, 2024.

2021). Other works include analyses of plain language versus legal language in controversial Indonesian laws (Marlia et al., 2023). An important milestone in this area was the Forum for Language Experts in the Police Force and Parliament, organized by the Community Development Center of *Badan Bahasa*, on August 27, 2015, at Hotel Park, Jakarta (Badan Pengembangan dan Pembinaan Bahasa, 2015). Discussions during the forum addressed topics such as the use of Indonesian language in drafting *Berita Acara Pemeriksaan* (ENG police investigation reports), issues of word and sentence structure, and challenges in legislative drafting. This highlights the significant contributions of language experts to institutions such as the police force and the House of Representatives (see also Dewan Perwakilan Rakyat RI, 2021).

Another milestone in the development of forensic linguistics in Indonesia is the contribution of institutions in hosting activities or launching products, services, or policies related to forensic linguistics. These contributions come from both higher education and non-higher education institutions. For the purposes of this Element, the explanation is divided into two sections as follows.

2.1.1 Development of Forensic Linguistics in Higher Education Institutions

As forensic linguistics continues to gain recognition and significance in Indonesia, universities and higher education institutions have begun incorporating this field into their curricula. Lecturers are disseminating forensic linguistics to students, actively conducting research, sharing their findings with local, national, and international audiences, and participating in community-based projects focused on forensic linguistics. The advancement of forensic linguistics in higher education aligns with the three primary functions of universities: teaching, research, and community service. To explore this development further, the authors conducted an extensive search, utilizing keywords in Indonesian such as *linguistik forensik Indonesia* (ENG forensic linguistics in Indonesia) and *kurikulum linguistik forensik* (ENG curriculum of forensic linguistics), and drawing on their own expertise and familiarity with the field.

In the area of teaching, forensic linguistics has been integrated into the curriculum at several universities in Indonesia since 2011. Although not yet available as a dedicated degree program, it is offered as a main or elective course, with credit hours ranging from two to twelve, across undergraduates, master's, and doctoral programs.

At the undergraduate level, forensic linguistics is typically offered as an elective course. For instance, the English Language and Literature program at Universitas Pendidikan Indonesia or UPI (ENG Indonesia University of

Education) includes a 4-credit course for students in their seventh semester (before new curriculum of 2024), while the Indonesian Language and Literature program at UPI offers a 2-credit course for sixth-semester students.[13] Additionally, UPI provides this course in a MOOC format via platforms such as WajarId[14] and Open University. Similarly, Universitas Pembangunan Nasional Veteran, East Java offers a 4-credit course to fifth-semester students in its linguistics program.[15] Other institutions incorporating forensic linguistics at the undergraduate level include Universitas Negeri Surabaya (a 2-credit course for fourth-semester students in the Indonesian Language and Literature program),[16] Universitas Diponegoro in Central Java,[17] and Universitas Jambi[18] (available in the Indonesian Literature program for 2 and 3-credit hours, respectively).

At the master's level, forensic linguistics is integrated as either an elective course or a specialization within linguistics programs. For example, Universitas Indonesia includes a 3-credit elective in forensic linguistics within its Linguistics program, while Universitas Nusa Cendana in Kupang[19] offers a similar 3-credit elective. Universitas Al Azhar Indonesia provides a more in-depth focus with a 12-credit concentration in its Applied Linguistics Master's Program, which includes courses like Language as Legal Evidence, Language in Judicial Processes, and Language in Legal Products.[20] At Universitas Brawijaya, forensic linguistics is part of the Linguistics Master's curriculum, alongside a 2-credit course in Legal and Business Translation.[21] Other institutions offering forensic linguistics in their Linguistics Master's programs include Universitas Padjadjaran,[22] Universitas Gadjah Mada (delivered via e-learning),[23] Universitas Negeri Yogyakarta,[24] and Universitas Mataram[25] in its Indonesian Language Education program and Universitas Warmadewa in its Linguistics Program.[26]

---

[13] https://indonesia.upi.edu/kurikulum-nondik/, accessed December 25, 2024.

[14] https://wajar.id/index.php/courses/pengantar-linguistik-forensik, accessed December 12, 2024

[15] https://drive.google.com/file/d/1sKrYRapKgNnuj34ZzVx0GpWJKRPy0gMU/view, accessed December 25, 2024.

[16] https://statik.unesa.ac.id/profileunesa_konten_statik/uploads/bakpk/file/c22979fc-b184-4a3c-bf63-e7c45de93af1.pdf, accessed December 25, 2024.

[17] https://sastraindonesia.fib.undip.ac.id/kurikulum/, accessed December 25, 2024.

[18] https://sastraindonesia.unja.ac.id/index.php/kurikulum-sastra-indonesia/, accessed December 25, 2024.

[19] https://linguistik.undana.ac.id/kurikulum/struktur-kurikulum/, accessed December 25, 2024.

[20] https://mlit.uai.ac.id/kurikulum-dan-sistem-perkuliahan/, accessed December 25, 2024.

[21] https://linguistics-fib.ub.ac.id/pendidikan/graduate-profil/, accessed December 25, 2024.

[22] https://fib.unpad.ac.id/program-pendidikan/ilmu-linguistik/, accessed December 25, 2024.

[23] https://elok.ugm.ac.id/course/index.php?categoryid=612, accessed December 25, 2024.

[24] https://s2pbsi.fbs.uny.ac.id/kurikulum, accessed 25 December, 2024.

[25] https://fkip.unram.ac.id/magisterbindo/mata-kuliah/, accessed December 25, 2024.

[26] https://pascasarjana.warmadewa.ac.id/page/mata-kuliah, accessed December 25, 2024.

At the doctoral level, forensic linguistics remains available as an elective option. For instance, UPI offers a 4-credit forensic linguistics course in its Doctoral Program of Linguistics.[27] Likewise, Universitas Pendidikan Ganesha features a 3-credit elective in forensic linguistics as part of its Doctoral Program in Language Education.[28] Other universities, including Universitas Negeri Jakarta (Applied Linguistics Doctoral Program),[29] Universitas Udayana,[30] and several others, also incorporate forensic linguistics into their doctoral curricula as elective courses.

To meet the demands of teaching and curriculum development, lecturers having a special interest in forensic linguistics have authored books in the field (Mahsun, 2018; Pastika & Puspani, 2021; Sholihatin, 2019; Subyantoro, 2022). Additionally, students have conducted research as part of course assignments or final projects (theses or dissertations) and published their findings in national or international journals (e.g. Adbaka & Datang, 2023; Haryanto & Arimi, 2022; Hermawan et al., 2021; Safitra et al., 2024).

The second key responsibility of lecturers is conducting research. As a relatively new field in Indonesia, forensic linguistics offers significant research gaps, providing ample opportunities for exploration and the potential to attract research funding. Moreover, given its critical role in addressing injustices through language analysis, research in forensic linguistics can contribute meaningfully to achieving Sustainable Development Goals (SDGs), particularly Goal 10 on reducing inequalities and Goal 16 on promoting peace, justice, and strong institutions. For instance, the authors of this Element received research funding from UPI in 2013 and 2014 (see Aziz et al., 2013, 2014). Additionally, Muniroh successfully obtained postdoctoral research funding in forensic linguistics, resulting in international journal publications. The first funding came from UPI's Visiting Fellow Scholarship program (July–August 2019), and the second from the Postdoctoral Program Awardee (September–December 2022) funded by the Ministry of Education, Culture, Research, and Technology of the Republic of Indonesia. Publications resulting from these grants appeared in high-ranking journals (see Muniroh & Heydon, 2022, 2024). Another example of funded research with outputs published in high-ranking journals is a study on person reference in police investigative interviews (see Vidhiasi et al., 2024). Another platform for lecturers to disseminate findings

---

[27] https://kurikulum.upi.edu/struktur/prodi/P507, accessed December 25, 2024.

[28] https://pasca.undiksha.ac.id/prodi/pendidikan-bahasa-s3/kurikulum/, accessed December 25, 2024.

[29] https://pps.unj.ac.id/profil-prodi-s3-pendidikanbahasa/, accessed December 25, 2024.

[30] https://s3linguistik.unud.ac.id/protected/storage/lampiran_page/93b4f7fd3d7a12f57f4bb26b bab20bf4.pdf, accessed December 25, 2024.

besides journal article publication is presenting in national or international conferences.

Currently, many national and international linguistic conferences hosted by universities and associations in Indonesia, such as KIMLI, CONAPLIN, KOLITA, and SEMANTIK, include or specifically call for papers on forensic linguistics. This growing interest has led to an increase in publications and scholarly discussions in the field. Universities have also shown a commitment to advancing forensic linguistics by organizing general or guest lectures featuring scholars from both local and international contexts.[31] Similarly, universities abroad have invited forensic linguistics scholars from Indonesia to share their expertise.[32] Collaboration among universities to host forensic linguistics events and discussions further highlights the growing recognition and importance of the field.[33]

Disseminating forensic linguistics through conferences also ties into the third key responsibility of lecturers: providing community service. In this capacity, academics aim to engage not only academic audiences but also the public including students, teachers, and law enforcement officers, raising awareness about forensic linguistics. Dissemination efforts often take the form of workshops or training sessions focused on the scopes of forensic linguistics offering solutions to societal problems. For example, these initiatives may involve educating participants about linguistic features in social media posts or expressions that could harm or offend others, potentially leading to legal issues. Such efforts address the increasing prevalence of language-based violence in digital media and schools, promoting preventive measures to mitigate these problems.[34] Another initiative involves providing training for police officers, prosecutors, and other law enforcement personnel to enhance their information-gathering skills while adhering to human rights and ethical standards.[35]

---

[31] See for example https://fib.ub.ac.id/a-guest-lecture-forensic-linguistics/, https://unmul.ac.id/news/antusias-peserta-mengikuti-kuliah-umum-linguistik-forensik-oleh-prof.-e.-aminudin-aziz,-m.a.,-ph.d., www.kemdikbud.go.id/main/blog/2022/10/beri-kuliah-tamu-di-unesa-kepala-badan-paparkan-peluang-linguistik-forensik-di-dunia-kerja, https://mli.fib.undip.ac.id/visiting-lecturer-mli-usung-tema-linguistik-forensik/, https://trisakti.ac.id/news/selisik-linguistik-forensik-dan-tinjauan-hukum-disinformasi-di-era-digital/, accessed December 26, 2024.

[32] See for example www.ust.edu.ph/wp-content/uploads/2020/12/Academia-December-1-30-2020_For-CB.pdf, https://ell.uol.edu.pk/event/graduate-seminar-series-gss/, www.manilatimes.net/2023/07/06/campus-press/ust-gathers-experts-on-forensic-legal-linguistics-in-iafll16/1899364, accessed December 26, 2024.

[33] See for example https://old.unimed.ac.id/2018/09/17/prodi-s3-ltbi-prodi-linguistik-usu-unnes-dan-ubl-kembangkan-linguistik-forensik/, accessed December 26, 2024.

[34] See for example https://berita.upi.edu/a-new-initiative-to-prevent-school-violence-in-bali/, https://berita.upi.edu/educational-collaboration-strengthens-ties-between-indonesia-and-the-philippines-three-key-events-successfully-concluded/, accessed December 26, 2024.

[35] See for example Hendrokumoro et al. (2019), www.linkedin.com/in/r-dian-dia-an-muniroh-9ab32638/recent-activity/all/, accessed December 26, 2024.

The growing recognition of forensic linguistics in universities is also evident in the establishment of centers for forensic linguistics[36] and dedicated journal platform for publication.[37] However, further support is needed to ensure the sustained development of these initiatives.

2.1.2 Development of Forensic Linguistics in Non-higher Education Institutions

Non-higher education institutions in this Element refer to *Badan Bahasa* (ENG the Agency for Language Development and Cultivation), *Badan Riset dan Inovasi Nasional* or BRIN (ENG The National Research and Innovation Agency), *Kepolisian Republik Indonesia* or Polri (ENG Indonesian National Police), *Badan Narkotika Nasional* or BNN (ENG National Narcotics Board), *Badan Pemeriksa Keuangan* or BPK (ENG The Audit Board of the Republic of Indonesia), *Komunitas Linguistik Forensik Indonesia* or KLFI (ENG Indonesian Forensic Linguistics Community), and *Himpunan Penerjemah Indonesia* or HPI (ENG The Association of Indonesian Translators). The following paragraphs detail their attention to forensic linguistics.

Providing forensic language analysis has been one of the primary services offered by *Badan Bahasa* for many years, though it was formally established as a program in 2015. This initiative stemmed from frequent requests from the Indonesian National Police to analyze language-related cases and provide expert testimonies. However, the language specialists at *Badan Bahasa* often lacked adequate training or knowledge in forensic linguistics, and there was no standardized approach for such work. To address this, *Badan Bahasa* published the *Guidelines for Forensic Linguistic Studies* (Khatimah & Kusumawardani, 2016).

In 2018, *Badan Bahasa* took another significant step by establishing the Forensic Linguistics Laboratory.[38] One of its flagship programs is *Bengkel Forensik Kebahasaan* (ENG the Workshop on Forensic Linguistics series), which has been conducted annually since its inception in 2018. The workshop covers topics such as language as evidence and language in police interviews. In 2019, it included a session on investigative interviewing, featuring Associate Professor Georgina Heydon, president of the International Association of Forensic Linguists, as a guest speaker. The workshops attract participants

---

[36] For example, Centre for Forensic Linguistics UPI (https://berita.upi.edu/upi-lahirkan-pusat-telisik-telaah-linguistik-forensik), Integrated Forensic Centres UI (https://lppsp.ui.ac.id/unit/forensik/?lang=id), Digital Forensics Centre Universitas Muhammadiyah Purwokerto (https://dfc.ump.ac.id/).

[37] See for example International Journal of Forensic Linguistics hosted by Universitas Warmadewa, Bali (www.ejournal.warmadewa.ac.id/index.php/ijfl).

[38] https://badanbahasa.kemdikbud.go.id/berita-detail/2792/badan-bahasa-akan-bentuk-laboratorium-forensik-linguistik, accessed December 26, 2024.

from various institutions, including the police, prosecutors, lawyers, cybercrime units, and immigration authorities.

Badan Bahasa has also addressed language-based crimes, such as by conducting research on cyberbullying among students in 2019 and 2020. In addition to disseminating findings to schools and relevant stakeholders, this research resulted in the publication of book chapters (Muniroh et al., 2022) and journal articles (e.g. Sukma et al., 2021). However, following the institutional transformation that required all research activities to fall under the National Research and Innovation Agency, *Badan Bahasa* was no longer allowed to conduct research directly.

Under Aziz's leadership, which began at *Badan Bahasa* in 2020,[39] the institution has placed greater emphasis on forensic linguistics, implementing strong programs for both internal and external audiences. The organization was restructured into specialized units known as *Kelompok Kepakaran dan Layanan Profesional* or KKLP (ENG Specialised-Expertise and Professional Services Groups). One of these groups is dedicated to Language Cultivation and Legal Services. Under this KKLP, training and workshops in forensic linguistics for internal staff have become more frequent and systematic, aiming to enhance their professionalism and expertise in service delivery. Other than its Main Office in the Capital, *Badan Bahasa* also has thirty regional representative offices across nearly all provinces in Indonesia, each mirroring the structure and programs of the main office in Jakarta. These regional offices actively work to improve staff capacity by organizing seminars and workshops, often collaborating with local universities[40] or inviting speakers from academic institutions and law enforcement agencies. This approach enables them to reach more diverse audiences and incorporate more authentic and varied materials into their programs.

In 2021, as a platform for disseminating research findings and studies, *Badan Bahasa* published the inaugural issue of *Jurnal Forensik Kebahasaan* (ENG the Journal of Forensic Linguistics).[41] In 2023, in response to the general election, which often features heated language disputes between parties, *Badan Bahasa* organized the Advanced Forensic Linguistics Class (Jakarta, October 8–14, 2023). This program was limited to fifteen participants who were required to demonstrate active English proficiency and provide a forensic linguistics portfolio. The class, led by experts from Aston University, United Kingdom Dr.

---

[39] https://badanbahasa.kemdikbud.go.id/sejarah, https://balaibahasajabar.kemdikbud.go.id/prof-e-aminudin-aziz-menjadi-kepala-badan-bahasa-2020-2024/, accessed December 27, 2024.

[40] https://unmul.ac.id/news/antusias-peserta-mengikuti-kuliah-umum-linguistik-forensik-oleh-prof.-e.-aminudin-aziz,-m.a.,-ph.d., accessed December 26, 2024.

[41] https://ojs.badanbahasa.kemdikbud.go.id/jurnal/index.php/jfk, accessed December 26, 2024.

Tahmineh Tayebi and Amy Booth along with specialists from *Badan Bahasa*, focused on advanced studies of hate speech within the field of forensic linguistics.[42] To disseminate the importance of language analytic skills and awareness for police officers, Aziz often gave special trainings for the police investigators at the regional police departments in conjunction with his regular visits to language regional offices.

Another institution that has shown interests in the development of forensic linguistics is BRIN (the National Research and Innovation Agency). As its name suggests, this agency serves as a hub for researchers across Indonesia. Forensic linguistics falls under the purview of the Research Centre for Language, Literature, and Community. Researchers who were previously affiliated with Badan Bahasa and had an interest in forensic linguistics have continued contributing to the field under their new roles at BRIN. For instance, research on authorship analysis utilizing a corpus linguistics approach has gained traction within the agency (Puspitasari, 2022; Puspitasari et al., 2023, 2025) as well as hate speech (Sanubarianto et al., 2023) and other issues in legal settings (Sukma et al., 2023). BRIN is also actively engaged in promoting forensic linguistics through webinars.[43]

The Indonesian National Police, through their *Puslitbang* (ENG Centre for Research and Development), has demonstrated significant attention to the field of forensic linguistics. Recognizing the critical role of language analysis in addressing language-based crimes, the authorities have undertaken notable initiatives to build capacity in this area. One such effort was an action research project aimed at enhancing police investigators' knowledge on forensic linguistics (see Azis, 2022). This initiative was prompted by the observation that language-based crimes are often not effectively addressed using forensic linguistic approaches due to several challenges. These include difficulties in accessing qualified forensic linguistics experts, particularly in *Polres* (ENG district police offices), and investigators' limited knowledge of the field. Additional challenges include insufficient IT infrastructure for investigating language-based crimes, inadequate familiarity with forensic linguistics tools and methodologies, budget constraints for investigative operations – especially in remote island regions, and a lack of skills to identify criminal speech or discourse and apply linguistic analysis in solving crimes.

To address these issues, the action research incorporated training to enhance investigators' knowledge and skills. The project was implemented across four

---

[42] https://kbi.kemdikbud.go.id/forensik.php, accessed December 27, 2024.

[43] See for example Samaya (2024), www.youtube.com/watch?v=LScTQaGf6Y0, www.youtube.com/watch?v=OgELjnZLxao, accessed December 26, 2024.

Polda (ENG regional police departments): East Nusa Tenggara,[44] North Sulawesi,[45] East Java,[46] and North Sumatera,[47] with thirty police investigators participating from each Polda. The training materials included an introduction to forensic linguistics theories, analytical models specific to language-based cases, authorship analysis techniques, and the application of forensic transcription. In this regard, participants engaged in case-based practicums and learned to use advanced tools such as ELAN (EUDICO Linguistic Annotator), PRAAT, AntConc (version 3.5.9), and AntWordProfiler (version 1.5.1). The research also involved a linguist as a consultant to guide the process.

The findings revealed significant insights. Many police investigators initially perceived language as merely a tool for communication, overlooking its potential role in facilitating or motivating crimes. They also struggled to differentiate between closely related language-based offenses, such as provocation, incitement, and hate speech. These challenges are not surprising, given the lack of formal training in forensic linguistics. These findings underscore the pressing need for systematic improvements in addressing language-based crimes in Indonesia. Key recommendations included (1) integration of forensic linguistics training as a core component of education and training programs for the Indonesian National Police, (2) expansion of the action research approach to all regional police departments to establish standardized practices for handling language-based crimes, and (3) establishment of databases on a Criminal Threat Assessment Database (CTAD) or a Criminally Oriented Communication Corpus (COCC) to support investigators with data-driven insights and case references. By implementing these recommendations, the Indonesian National Police can enhance the capacity of its law enforcement personnel to address the complexities of language-based crimes effectively.

As highlighted earlier in this Element, issues of injustice frequently occur within the realm of law enforcement. It is commendable that law enforcement institutions, such as the Indonesian National Police and the National Narcotics Board, have hosted investigative interviewing training sessions and invited forensic linguists, including Muniroh and Aziz, to contribute. These initiatives provide opportunities for forensic linguists to enhance police interviews from a linguistic perspective, although such training is not conducted regularly. In this

---

[44] https://tribratanewsntt.com/polda-ntt-gelar-riset-aksi-tentang-peningkatan-kemampuan-linguistik-forensik, accessed December 28, 2024.

[45] https://manado.antaranews.com/berita/119569/puslitbang-polri-melakukan-riset-aksi-peningkatan-kemampuan-penyidik, accessed December 28, 2024.

[46] https://kumparan.com/humas-polres-situbondo/polri-lakukan-penelitian-gasbin-tingkatkan-kemampuan-ilmu-linguistik-penyidik-1vHfFFs1lGS/full, accessed December 26, 2024.

[47] http://120.29.228.217:8080/blog/berita-2/post/riset-aksi-penguatan-kemampuan-linguistik-forensik-di-polda-sumatera-utara-2468, accessed December 28, 2024.

regard, forensic linguistics provides valuable insights not only for addressing language-based crimes but also for improving police officers' interviewing competencies.

Another key institution in Indonesia that supports law enforcement efforts, while operating independently, is Badan Pemeriksa Keuangan or BPK (ENG the Audit Board of the Republic of Indonesia). BPK's primary mandate is auditing financial statements and ensuring accountability in the use of public funds. Notably, BPK has engaged with forensic linguistics through investigative interviewing training. In this context, Muniroh contributed to developing the SANTAI investigative model, adopted by BPK. This model integrates international research and policy insights to enhance best practices.[48]

Badan Pengawas Pemilu or Bawaslu (ENG General Election Supervisory Agency) is another institution that has actively used expertise of forensic linguists for its mission purposes. As an independent entity, Bawaslu functions to supervise general elections at all levels: national, provincial, and municipal/regency. To avoid or minimize the potential of black campaigns that include insults, defamations, and other kinds of hate speech by candidates, Bawaslu sets up forums for its supervisory teams involving police officers and attorneys by inviting forensic linguists to give their insights. Aziz has always become one of the speakers in the forums.

Worth mentioning in this Element that also have contributed to the dissemination of forensic linguistics is The Indonesian Forensic Linguistics Community (KLFI),[49] founded by Susanto on November 3, 2014. It serves as a platform for discussing and sharing knowledge about forensic linguistics in Indonesia. This learning community has brought together enthusiasts from across the country and organizes online annual international conferences. These conferences often feature prominent figures in forensic linguistics, from the UK, Europe, Australia, the United States, and Asia, including Indonesia, and law enforcement authorities.

Himpunan Penerjemah Indonesia or HPI (ENG The Association of Indonesian Translators) is the other non-higher education institution discussed in this Element. As the primary professional body for translation and interpreting in Indonesia, HPI has significantly contributed to the field of legal interpreting and the translation of legal documents. To enhance competencies in legal interpreting, HPI has organized various training initiatives, including a webinar on ethics in interpreting (covering police and court contexts),[50] a session on

---

[48] See www.youtube.com/watch?v=1kpW0RM06Pw&t=4s, accessed December 26, 2024.

[49] https://klfi.weebly.com/, accessed December 25, 2024.

[50] www.hpi.or.id/ethics-in-interpreting-police-and-court, accessed December 29, 2024.

court interpreting procedures,[51] and specialized training on translating court documents.[52] HPI also offers a Directory of Indonesian Translators and Interpreters, featuring filters for profession (translator, interpreter, or both), language pairs (encompassing foreign languages like English and European and Asian languages, as well as local languages), and areas of specialization (such as law enforcement, legal contracts, and general legal contexts). This resource simplifies access for individuals and professionals seeking relevant translation and interpreting services. While HPI is not officially recognized as a certification authority, it has conducted certification exams in multiple languages over the past two decades (Infotek HPI, 2024). Notably, HPI member I Gede Bhisma Griwanasta has established agreements with law enforcement bodies, including Religious Courts in Denpasar, Badung, and Gianyar in Bali Province, to provide courtroom interpreting services when required.[53]

This concludes the section on the origins, early influences, and key milestones of forensic linguistics in Indonesia, highlighting the contributions of both individuals and institutions to its development. The following section explores how scholars in Indonesia engage with forensic linguistics. This discussion is crucial for triangulating the active roles of academics, higher education institutions, and nonacademic organizations in disseminating forensic linguistics across the country.

2.2 First Encounter with Forensic Linguistics

This section describes how scholars in Indonesia encounter forensic linguistics, drawing parallels with the trajectories of leading international scholars – such as Eades, Ainsworth, Coulthard, Finegan, Gibbons, and Shuy, whose influential work over several decades has helped shape the field. Their reflections, featured in a 2021 volume of the *Language and Law/Linguagem e Direito* dedicated to "how I got started as a forensic linguist," offer valuable insights into the development of forensic linguistics and the diverse entry points scholars have taken into the discipline (Coulthard & Sousa-Silva, 2021).

According to responses from fifty-three participants to the question, "How did you first encounter forensic linguistics?" the results suggest that scholars have diverse initial encounters with forensic linguistics, primarily through academic

---

[51] www.hpi.or.id/court-interpreting-pemahaman-tata-cara-pelaksanaan-tugas-juru-bahasa-di-pen gadilan, accessed December 29, 2024.

[52] www.hpi.or.id/new/pelatihan-penerjemahan-dokumen-pengadilan-bahasa-indonesia-bahasa-inggris/, accessed December 29, 2024.

[53] https://pa-denpasar.go.id/index.php/publikasi/arsip-artikel/246-perjanjian-kerja-sama-antara-pengadilan-agama-denpasar-dengan-penerjemah-bahasa-asing-27-april-2021, https://pta-mataram.go.id/berita-agama/876-wujudkan-pelayanan-prima-pengadilan-agama-badung-jalin-kerja-sama-dengan-penerjemah-bahasa-asing

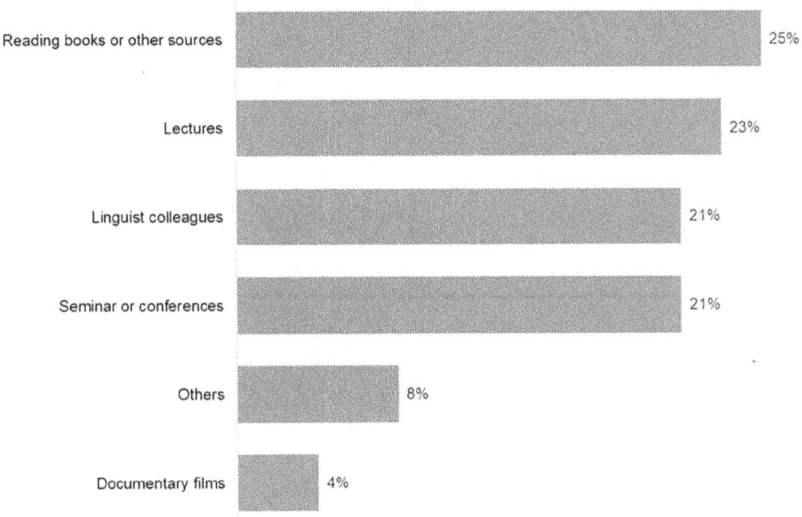

Figure 4 First encounter with forensic linguistics.

and professional channels such as reading books or other sources (25%), attending lectures (23%), interacting with linguist colleagues (21%), and participating in seminars or conferences (21%). This indicates the significant role of formal education, professional networks, and academic events in introducing individuals to the field. Lesser influences include other methods (8%) and documentary films (4%), showing that diverse media and experiences can also spark interest in forensic linguistics. This distribution is illustrated in Figure 4.

A follow-up question regarding their motivation to study forensic linguistics reveals a range of driving factors. Participants are motivated by curiosity about persuasive language dynamics (18%), involvement in language analysis for legal cases (15%), a desire for research and academic pursuits (15%), fascination with complex crime narratives (14%), a commitment to justice enhancement (14%), interest in lectures on language analysis (12%), career aspirations in the legal field (9%), other motivations (2%), and personal experiences in crime (1%). The distribution of these motivations is illustrated in Figure 5.

These findings contrast with the experiences of leading international scholars in forensic linguistics. While many participants in the study were motivated by academic interests and specific career goals, renowned scholars often began their careers in forensic linguistics through unexpected or unplanned events. For instance, some were approached by lawyers (e.g. Eades, 2021), colleagues (e.g. Coulthard, 2021), solicitors (e.g. Gibbons, 2021), or attorneys (e.g. Finegan, 2021) seeking their linguistic expertise for specific legal cases. The differences

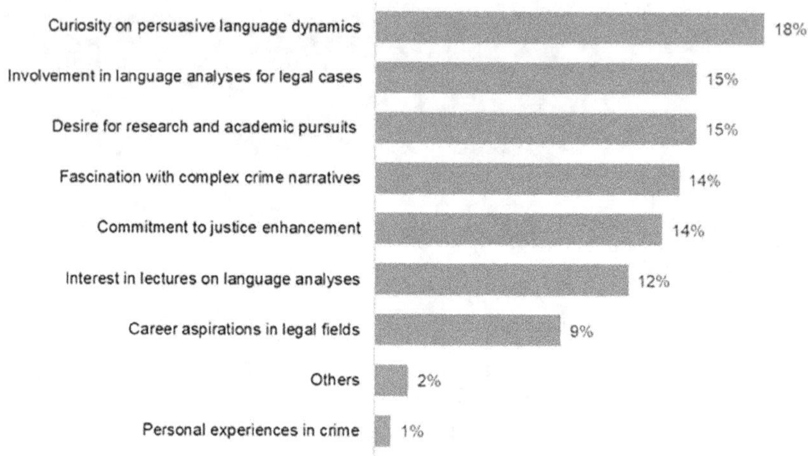

Figure 5 Motivation to study forensic linguistics.

might reflect the development of forensic linguistics in the world which now has been acknowledged as a mature discipline (see Coulthard et al., 2021).

Another interesting finding from the survey reveals a range of similarities between the experiences of participants and those of leading international scholars. For instance, many scholars such as Gibbons (2021), Coulthard (2021), and Shuy (2021) have a background in linguistics. Additionally, several have transitioned from other areas, such as literature or language education, to forensic linguistics, mirroring Ainsworth's (2021) path. As illustrated in Figure 6, the participants' educational backgrounds are predominantly in Indonesian language, literature, or education (49%), followed by linguistics including applied linguistics and forensic linguistics (38%). A smaller percentage come from English language, literature, or education (8%), unmentioned fields (4%), and classical Javanese literature (2%).

Almost half of the participants perceived their educational background as relevant to forensic linguistics. Among these, half reported attending forensic linguistic training, specifically organized by the Agency for Language Development and Cultivation of the Republic of Indonesia and the Integrated Forensic Centre of the University of Indonesia. The other half stated that although their educational background was not directly relevant, they received additional training in the field. There is a growing number of Indonesians pursuing postgraduate degrees in forensic linguistics, at universities in Indonesia which have either an academic major or offer courses in forensic linguistics (e.g. Universitas Pendidikan Indonesia, University of Indonesia, North Sumatra University) or abroad (e.g. in Australia, the United Kingdom).

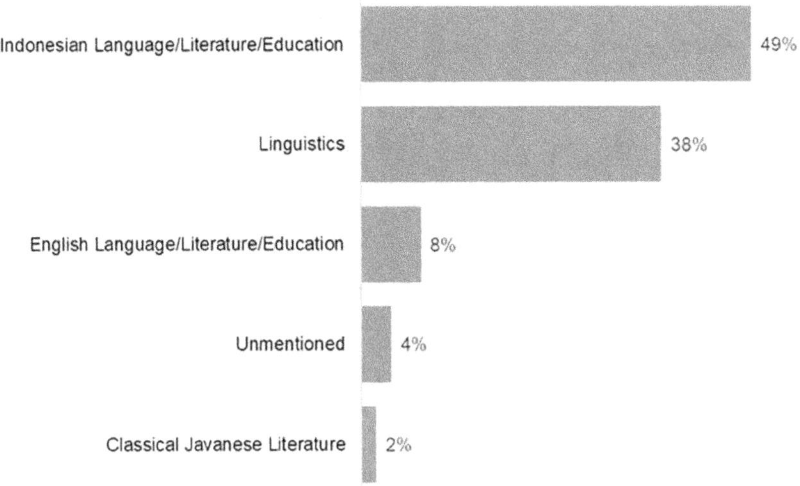

Figure 6 Participants' educational background.

With the aforementioned educational backgrounds, the participants work as language experts in governmental offices (66%), academics (23%), unspecified fields (6%), and researchers (6%) (Figure 7). Among those working as language experts in governmental offices, 71 percent have experience analyzing language for courtroom purposes. Specifically, they are involved in providing expert analysis on language-related crimes, including insults, defamation, hate speech, fake news, and cases involving the problems of land deeds. In contrast, only 45 percent of the academic participants have experience conducting research in forensic linguistics and providing expert opinions in legal contexts. Notably, none of the researchers surveyed have practical experience in analyzing language as evidence. These results point to the critical application of forensic linguistics in government and legal contexts in Indonesia, while also identifying areas where academic and research involvement in practical forensic linguistics could be expanded.

As discussed in the previous section, both authors of this Element are academics who entered the field of forensic linguistics through academic and professional pathways. Muniroh was introduced to forensic linguistics in 2002 during a sociolinguistics class as part of her bachelor's degree in English Language Education. Aziz began his journey in the field while pursuing a doctoral degree in linguistics at Monash University in 1997, reflecting a trend observed among the majority of survey participants. However, it is important to acknowledge earlier scholars, such as Lukman Hakim, who provided testimony in 1995. Similar to experiences described by Coulthard and Eades in their early

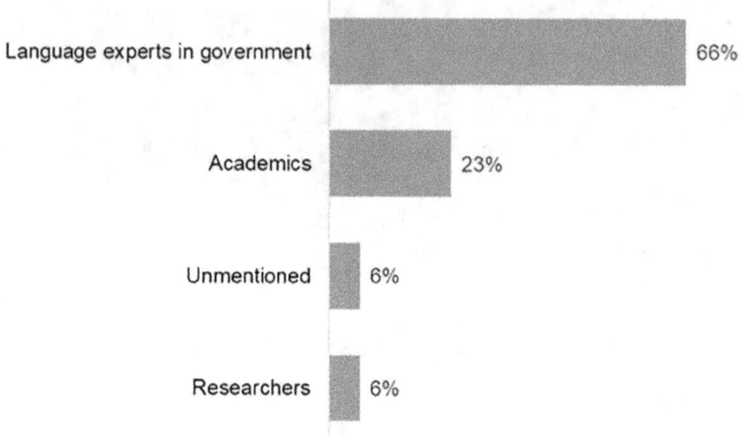

Figure 7 Participants' profession.

cases, these pioneers often entered forensic linguistics without prior exposure to the discipline, relying instead on their broader linguistic expertise. The next section provides an overview of the key characteristics of forensic linguistics in Indonesia.

2.3 Characteristics of Forensic Linguistics in Indonesia

Indonesia, a nation characterized by its diverse social landscape, has witnessed a growing academic interest in forensic linguistics. Alongside this, universities and government institutions have become increasingly engaged in promoting and advancing the field. These developments position Indonesia to contribute significantly to the global achievement of sustainable development goals through the practical application of forensic linguistics.

This section explores the defining characteristics of forensic linguistics in the country. By understanding these attributes, stakeholders can identify emerging needs, address existing gaps, and provide targeted support to further develop the discipline, ensuring its impact is both meaningful and far-reaching. There are three main characteristics of forensic linguistics in Indonesia:

1) Many scholars practicing forensic linguistics enter the field from broader linguistic backgrounds, gaining expertise through experience, research, and specialized training to address forensic contexts, rather than through specialized master's or doctoral degrees in forensic linguistics.

This reflects the interdisciplinary and applied nature of the field, where expertise in areas like phonetics, morphology, syntax, semantics, pragmatics, sociolinguistics, and discourse analysis can be effectively applied depending on the linguistic challenges presented by a case. Moreover, the judicial system does not currently mandate that forensic linguists hold specialized master's or doctoral degrees in forensic linguistics. While such degrees provide tailored knowledge and skills that are undoubtedly beneficial, universities in Indonesia have not yet introduced comprehensive master's or doctoral programs dedicated solely to forensic linguistics. Nonetheless, an increasing number of scholars, often supported by scholarships, are pursuing advanced degrees in forensic linguistics at universities in the United Kingdom and Australia, thereby contributing to the growing academic and professional expertise in the field. Additionally, some scholars practicing forensic linguistics opt to obtain formal degrees in law, either at the bachelor's or master's level, to gain a stronger grasp of legal perspectives. This interdisciplinary knowledge enhances their ability to collaborate effectively with legal professionals.

The importance of both linguistic expertise and contextual knowledge is underscored by notable cases in Indonesia. Heryanto (1995) critiques the analysis by Drs. Lukman Hakim in the case of alleged insults by Permadi, where the interpretation of the words *otoriter* (ENG authoritarian) and *diktator* (ENG dictator) relied solely on dictionary definitions. Heryanto argued that such an approach failed to capture the nuanced meanings of the terms within their specific contexts. Similarly, Mahsun (2018) highlights the challenges in the Ahok blasphemy case, where divergent linguistic analyses demonstrated the complexity of applying linguistic frameworks to legal contexts without formal forensic linguistics training.

This trend is also evident in legal interpreting. Many interpreters assisting in legal settings possess proficiency in the required languages but lack formal training or certification as legal interpreters. Tampubolon (2024), building on Hale's works (2011, 2019), emphasizes that interpreters need skills that extend beyond bilingual fluency. These include four essential areas of competence: linguistic and discursive abilities, contextual understanding, interpreting expertise, and interactional proficiency.

In Indonesia, with its diverse local languages and growing influx of expatriates and tourists, the role of interpreters is critical, as their presence directly impacts the resolution of legal cases. In response to this need, law enforcement institutions, such as courts, have established memoranda of understanding with professional legal interpreters. In contrast, some courts rely on local staff who speak the relevant languages, or those with a background in foreign languages such as English, to serve as interpreters. This practice also extends to the police, prosecutors, and lawyers, who often have to resort to non-professional interpreters.

These examples illustrate the potential and limitations of scholars entering the field with broader language or linguistic expertise. While their contributions are valuable, the evolving demands of forensic linguistics emphasize the need for specialized training, education, and standardized approaches to address complex language-based legal challenges effectively.

2) The use of language as evidence has gained significant prominence, largely driven by growing demands from the justice sector.

This trend is rooted in several key historical and societal shifts: the early influence of language-based crimes during the Old Era, where restrictions on freedom of expression often led to imprisonment; the societal transition from communal structures to a more individualistic focus, emphasizing personal dignity; Indonesia's rich history of oral traditions; and the shift from face-to-face interactions to digital-mediated communication. These factors collectively highlight the evolving role of language in both societal dynamics and legal contexts as well as the increasing prevalence of language-based crimes in recent years.

Let us examine some crime data from Indonesia. According to the original data accessed from the National Crime Information Center[54] on June 20, 2024, covering the years 2022–2024, the total number of crimes in Indonesia is 1,056,234. From the comprehensive dataset, we have identified the top ten types of crimes in Indonesia (see Figure 8). The highest number of crimes is aggravated theft with 126,174 cases, followed by traffic accidents with 115,805 cases, and persecution with 105,090 cases. Lower on the list are fraud with 102,616 cases, regular theft with 99,972 cases, narcotics with 91,449 cases, motor vehicle theft with 43,402 cases, embezzlement with 35,218 cases, beating with 32,786 cases, and criminal acts in child protection with 27,780 cases. In such cases, forensic linguistics in a broad definition can provide valuable insights to support police interviews and other related legal processes and enhance the overall understanding and resolution of these cases.

Meanwhile, the types of crime that often rely on language-based evidence were identified to appear lower on the list. These include threats (10,038 cases), forgery of authentic letters (6817 cases), defamation (5480 cases), insults (3028 cases), and blackmail and threats (2964 cases) (other types of cases can be seen in Figure 9). It is true that the number of cases sits on the lower positions, yet such number has sparked the need of forensic linguists to take part in the legal processes. Many studies relevant to these have been conducted by Indonesian

---

[54] https://pusiknas.polri.go.id/data_kejahatan, accessed September 4, 2024.

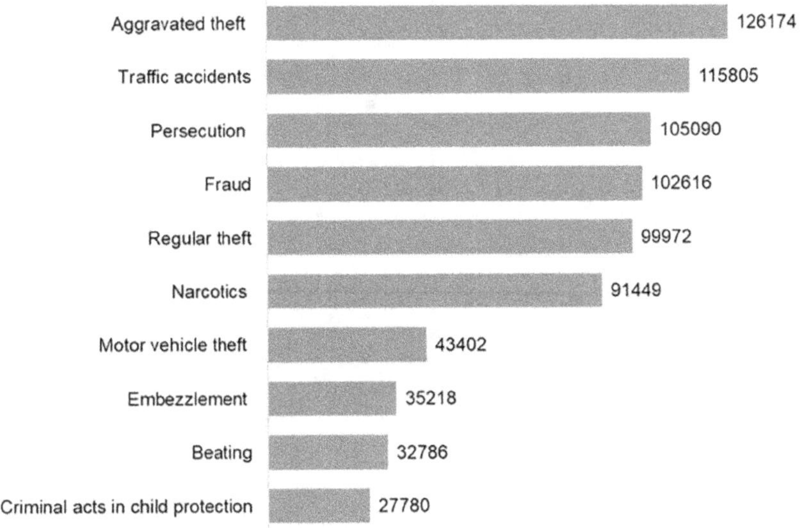

Figure 8 Top ten types of crime during 2022–2024.

scholars and examples of linguistic analysis for the purposes of case investigation are provided in Section 4.

Crimes that heavily rely on language-based evidence were found to be less frequently represented in the research literature despite their high incidence (see Figure 9 for a complete list of crime types). While Indonesian scholars have conducted research on these crimes, and Section 3 provides examples of forensic linguistic research, there appears to be an imbalance in research focus. For instance, despite threats being a significant area of concern, with high demand for forensic linguist testimony as indicated by the high number of cases (Figure 9), research on threatening communication appears to be underrepresented in the literature. Similarly, research investigating forgery or authorship is relatively rare. This gap in the literature presents a significant area for future research and scholarly contribution.

By leveraging the expertise of forensic linguists, legal professionals can delve deeper into the linguistic nuances, uncover hidden meanings, and strengthen the overall investigation and prosecution of these cases. In this regard, forensic linguists can assist in areas like the analysis of verbal and written evidence, the interpretation of idiomatic expressions and cultural references, and the identification of authorship. By integrating linguistic expertise into the legal process, professionals can make more informed decisions and ensure a more thorough and fair investigation and adjudication of these crimes.

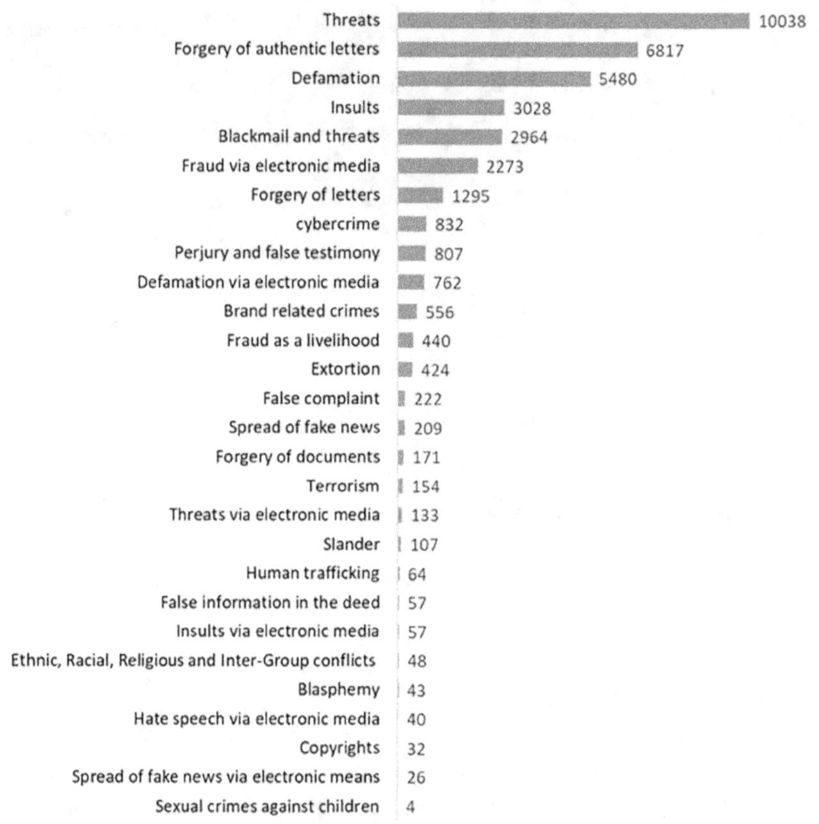

Figure 9 Types of crime relying on language as evidence during 2020–2024.

3) As authoritative figures, linguists have gained reputable recognition and expansion of forensic linguistics in Indonesia.

Many linguists practicing forensic linguistics in Indonesia occupy influential leadership positions at universities or national organizations. With their capabilities and academic authorities, they play pivotal roles in developing relevant programs to support forensic linguistics and securing funding for the initiatives. This is particularly evident in the work of those serving as presidents of forensic linguistics associations or directors of language-related centers in universities, where their primary responsibilities align with advancing forensic linguistics.

One notable figure is E. Aminudin Aziz, who, as the head of the MLI Branch at UPI and vice rector for Planning, Research, and Development at UPI, facilitated the success of KIMLI 2011 by inviting Dr. Georgina Heydon, a prominent forensic linguist from Australia. Furthermore, in his capacity as the head of the Agency for Language Development and Cultivation since 2020, forensic linguistics has become integrated into more systematic programs and has been disseminated through representative offices across the archipelago in line with the institution vision and mission.

4)	The introduction of forensic linguistics in bachelor's degree programs at universities reflects the growing academic recognition and development of the field, offering early exposure to students and supporting its continued expansion within academia.

There is a common misconception among law enforcement officers that anyone with a background in language or linguistics is automatically qualified to practice forensic linguistics. This view overlooks the specialized training and expertise required in the field, which goes beyond core areas of linguistics and combines linguistic depth with context-specific competence. Such training often includes skills in forensic linguistic analysis, authorship attribution, expert witness report writing, communicating findings to legal audiences, and analyzing the pragmatics of legal texts and spoken evidence.

Additionally, the rising prevalence of social media conflicts leading to legal repercussions highlights a lack of digital literacy and language awareness among the public. To address these issues, increasing early academic exposure to forensic linguistics is crucial. This is evident in the development of courses on forensic linguistics as introduction in bachelor's degree in some universities in Indonesia. Such exposure can raise awareness about the societal and legal impact of language use and misuse while demonstrating how studying linguistics can contribute to enhancing the delivery of justice in the country. Furthermore, these courses broaden students' academic and career pathways, encouraging them to pursue advanced studies in forensic linguistics.

This early academic exposure in Indonesia has encouraged students, lecturers, and researchers to publish journal articles in the field of forensic linguistics, contributing to a broader scope for linguistics conferences in the country. The following section explores the trends in research gaps, theoretical frameworks, and concepts within Indonesian forensic linguistic analysis.

3 Forensic Linguistic Research in Indonesia

The growth of forensic linguistics in Indonesia has been shaped by contributions from students and scholars trained domestically and abroad, influencing research nationally and internationally. To map publications, the authors used Publish or Perish and Google Scholar to search works from 2011 to 2023 with five keywords: forensic linguistics, language and law, language as evidence, legal linguistics, and Indonesia (accessed on March 15, 2024). The period begins in 2011, a milestone year for the field, and covers a decade to capture publication trends. A manual review of journals and conference proceedings complemented the keyword search.

To check for recent developments, the authors searched Scopus and Web of Science for 2024 publications (accessed on August 7, 2025) using similar keywords. None were found in Web of Science, and only five in Scopus, mostly on established themes, such as language in legal processes (see Anisah & Sari, 2024; Muniroh & Heydon, 2024) and language as evidence (see Mardikantoro & Yuniawan, 2024; Mubarok et al., 2024). One notable exception was found to apply forensic linguistics to Sharia law in Aceh (see Yusuf et al., 2024). These findings support focusing on the 2011–2023 time frame for a consistent and representative overview.

Given potential overlaps in keyword search results for 2011–2023 publications, the authors carefully identified and removed or merged duplicates. After data reduction, a total of 298 publications were included in the analysis. This encompassed a diverse range of sources, including Scopus-indexed journals, international journals not indexed in Scopus, SINTA-accredited journals, national journals not accredited in SINTA, international conference proceedings, and other relevant publications such as books/book chapters and theses/ dissertations.

As we can see in Figure 10, this distribution reveals that SINTA-accredited journals (36%) were the most common publication venue for forensic linguistics research in Indonesia, followed by international conference proceedings

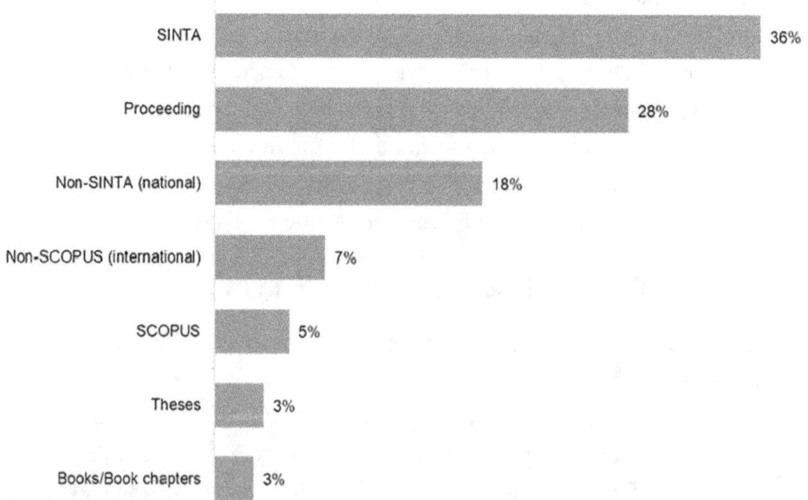

Figure 10 Types of publication.

(28%) and national journals not accredited in SINTA (18%). International journals not indexed in Scopus (7%) and Scopus-indexed journals (5%) accounted for a smaller proportion of publications. Books/book chapters and theses/dissertations constituted the smallest proportion, each representing 3 percent of the total.

This finding can be partly explained by the academic requirements for students in many Indonesian universities. For example, at our university, undergraduate students have the option of completing their studies through either a traditional thesis pathway or by publishing an article in a national journal. While publication is optional, those who choose the publication pathway must submit evidence of their article having been submitted to a journal indexed at least at the SINTA 6 level, or they must provide proof of publication (both print and digital copies) in a journal indexed at least at the SINTA 6 level.

For master's and doctoral students, scientific publication is a mandatory requirement. Master's students must fulfil one of the following criteria: they must have one article accepted for publication (accepted status) in a nationally accredited journal with a minimum SINTA 3 rating or in an international journal, or they must have presented at least one scientific paper at an international seminar. For master's students aiming for a cum laude grade (equivalent to First Class Honours), which typically requires a GPA of 3.76 or higher out of 4.0, the publication requirements are often more stringent. These students are frequently required to publish their research in international conference proceedings indexed by Scopus or Web of Science, or in SINTA 2-ranked journals.

Doctoral students typically need to fulfil the following: they must have one article accepted for publication (accepted status) in a reputable international journal indexed by Scopus or Web of Science, and they must have an article published (published status) in the proceedings of a reputable international seminar indexed by Scopus or Web of Science. Alternatively, they can fulfill this requirement by having an article accepted for publication (accepted status) in a nationally accredited journal with a minimum SINTA 3 rating. However, for doctoral students aspiring to graduate with a cum laude grade, they are typically required to publish one article in a Q2 Scopus-indexed journal or two articles in Q3 Scopus-indexed journals as part of their degree requirements.

This emphasis on publication within the academic system, particularly in SINTA-accredited journals and conference proceedings, likely contributes to the high proportion of publications in national journals and conference proceedings. The lower occurrence of publications in books or book chapters can be explained by the fact that publications in books or book chapters may hold less weight in academic promotion compared to Scopus-indexed journal articles.

These publications were then categorized into four research areas of forensic linguistics: "language and the law," "language in the legal processes," "language as evidence," and "language education and law." Additionally, a category labeled "others" was included to accommodate publications that did not neatly fit within the other four categories. Data from books and book chapters were excluded from the analysis as they primarily focused on descriptive accounts and lacked specific theories, concepts, or methodologies.

As shown in Table 1, research on "language as evidence" constituted the largest proportion (61.03%), followed by "language in legal processes" (15.17%) and "others" (11.72%). "Language and the law" (10.34%) and "language education and law" (1.72%) comprised the smallest proportions. This finding is in line with the historical and sociocultural conditions of Indonesia as discussed in Section 1.

Across all publication platforms, research in these four areas was predominantly published in national journals accredited in SINTA, followed by conference proceedings or national journals not accredited in SINTA. Notably, while "language as evidence" generally dominates research, an interesting observation in Scopus-indexed publications is a higher proportion of research in "language and legal processes" compared to "language as evidence," although this difference is not statistically significant. The high number of articles published in national journals demonstrate the growing interest of Indonesian journals in these topics. Additionally, the increasing number of presentations at international conferences indicates a growing interest in forensic linguistics research within the Indonesian academic community. Other reasons have been explained in the previous paragraph related to academic requirements in universities.

It is generally perceived that publishing in a SINTA 1 journal indicates high-quality research, often equated to the level of quality expected in Scopus-indexed journals. However, it is important to note that while SINTA 1 signifies a high standard within the Indonesian academic context, it does not automatically guarantee inclusion in Scopus, which has its own rigorous indexing criteria. Given the relatively low number of publications by Indonesian scholars in international forensic linguistics research, several factors might contribute to this. Firstly, language barriers pose a significant challenge, as publishing in international journals requires high-quality English writing. Secondly, some research may not yet meet the stringent international standards for publication in Scopus-indexed journals, which often have rigorous requirements for research methodology, data analysis, and theoretical frameworks. Lastly, a lack of international collaboration can hinder research quality and reduce the likelihood of publication in international journals.

Table 1 Distribution of forensic linguistic research areas across publication platforms

Research Areas	SCOPUS	Non-SCOPUS (International)	SINTA	Non-SINTA (National)	Proceeding	Theses	COUNT	Percentage
Language as evidence	4	14	71	29	53	6	177	61.03%
Language in legal processes	5	5	15	4	12	3	44	15.17%
Others	2	2	9	11	10	0	34	11.72%
Language and the law	2	1	12	8	6	1	30	10.34%
Language education and law	2	0	1	1	1	0	5	1.72%
Total	15	22	108	53	82	10	290	100.00%

The distribution of the publications across the various publication platforms is given in Table 1.

The following subsections provide a detailed analysis of the publications, including an exploration of the trends in linguistic theories and concepts relevant to forensic linguistics in Indonesia, the methodological approaches employed, and the interdisciplinary approaches adopted within the field in Indonesia.

3.1 Linguistic Theories and Concepts

The most significant contributions of forensic linguistics research in Indonesia concern "language as evidence," reaching audiences both domestically and internationally through publications in Indonesian and English. An analysis of 177 publications revealed fifteen distinct forensic case types. The five most prevalent cases were hate speech (27%), defamation (17%), insult (15%), fake news (9%), and suicide notes (8%) (see Table 2). Other identified cases included cyberbullying, blasphemy, sexual harassment/abuse, incitement, forensic speaker analysis, trademark disputes, threatening communication, bribery, fraud, and murder. The observed distribution of case types and their frequencies is not surprising, given the historical and sociopolitical context of Indonesia as discussed in Section 1.

While most forensic case studies were published in national journals accredited in SINTA, followed by conference proceedings and national journals not accredited in SINTA, some appeared in international journals. These included topics on hate speech, defamation, insult, fake news, suicide notes, and blasphemy, albeit in smaller quantities. Notably, only four case types – defamation, suicide notes, cyberbullying, and blasphemy – were found in Scopus-indexed journal publications. The distribution of these cases across various publication platforms is presented in Table 2.

An analysis of publications from 2011 to 2023 revealed that research in this area primarily employed concepts and frameworks drawn from semantics and pragmatics. Although theories on functional grammar, critical discourse analysis, computer-mediated discourse, and phonetics/phonology were also adopted, their application was less frequent. The following examples highlight some of the most prominent approaches.

1) Lexical and grammatical semantics

   Antara (2023) employed a lexical–grammatical semantics framework to analyze a statement by Dayu Gayatri on the *Chanel Palace* YouTube channel (2021), in which she allegedly defamed *Perhimpunan Pemuda*

Table 2 Types of cases in forensic linguistics research

No	Forensic cases	SCOPUS	Non-SCOPUS (International)	SINTA	Non-SINTA (National)	Proceeding	Theses	COUNT	Percentage
1.	Hate speech		6	22	7	12	1	48	27%
2.	Defamation	1	3	15	5	5	1	30	17%
3.	Insult		1	10	6	9	1	27	15%
4.	Fake news		1	5	1	8	1	16	9%
5.	Suicide notes	1	2	4	3	4		14	8%
6.	Cyberbullying	1		4	1	6	1	13	7%
7.	Blasphemy	1	1	2	1	3		8	5%
8.	Sexual harassment or abuse			5	1			6	3%
9.	Incitement			2	1	2	1	6	3%
10.	Forensic speaker verification			1	2	2		5	3%
11.	Trademark/disputed meanings			1	1	2		4	2%
12.	Threatening communication			3				3	2%
13.	Bribery			1				1	1%
14.	Fraud			1				1	1%
15.	Murder			1				1	1%
Total		4	14	71	29	53	6	177	100%

Hindu or Peradah (ENG Hindu Youth Association) by claiming it was affiliated with Vishva Hindu Parishad, categorized as a terrorist organization. Similar frameworks have been used in other studies on defamation (e.g. Amin & Burhanuddin, 2021; Mintowati, 2016) and hate speech (e.g. Tarigan & Mulyadi, 2019).

2) Speech acts

Sarifuddin et al. (2021) applied speech act theory to analyze alleged incitement by Natalius Pigai on YouTube, where he claimed that Indonesia's president and vice president are always from Java, implying that people from other islands serve only as subordinates. Similar approaches have been used in research on hate speech. Similar framework have been used in other studies on hate speech (e.g. Ria & Setiawan, 2023; Suryani et al., 2021), defamation (e.g. Halid, 2022), insult (e.g. Karenisa, 2020), cyberbullying (e.g. Syahid et al., 2022), and blasphemy (e.g. Pastika, 2019).

3) Conversational implicatures or cooperative principles

Radfar et al. (2020) applied Grice's theory of conversational implicature to analyze recorded conversations related to the murder of Jamal Khashoggi.

4) Relevance theory

Ilzam (2019) analyzed a suicide note by a married young woman to identify its underlying motive.

5) Politeness

Subyantoro et al. (2023) applied Culpeper's impoliteness framework to analyze cyberbullying comments on Instagram targeting Indonesian celebrity. A similar framework has been applied in studies on hate speech (e.g. Manik et al., 2022; Widiantho, 2020).

6) Critical discourse analysis

Thamrin et al. (2023) employed Fairclough's (1995) critical discourse analysis framework to examine fake news as found in Supreme Court decisions on fake news through the categories of representation, relations, identity, and sociocultural practices. This framework has also been employed in other studies on defamation (e.g. Kusno, 2021) and hoaks (e.g. Arianto, 2021).

7) Transitivity analysis

> Rifki et al. (2021) examined process types in email fraud through the transitivity system, finding a predominant use of material processes to create misleading statements and false authority figures aimed at deceiving and persuading recipients. A similar framework has been applied in studies on suicide notes (e.g. Ridhwani & Sawirman, 2020; Sujatna & Sujatna, 2020).

8) Appraisal theory

> Adbaka and Datang (2023) applied appraisal theory to analyze an alleged defamation case in which a Probolinggo civil servant claimed the Regional People's Representative Council (DPRD) had lower social status than local sex workers. Other studies applying appraisal theory have examined hate speech (e.g. Bachari, 2019; Syahid et al., 2021).

Research on hate speech in Indonesia has predominantly employed frameworks such as lexical semantics, pragmatic speech acts, politeness theory (encompasses the notion of impoliteness), and appraisal theory. These approaches were highlighted in the in-depth study by Sirulhaq, Yuwono, and Muta'ali (2023). The data for their research were analyzed using a CALL (computer-assisted language learning) approach, integrating NVivo 12 software with Lancs Box 6.0. Articles were drawn from all Indonesian publications indexed in DOAJ and Google Scholar without restrictions on publication year. A total of forty-four articles related to hate speech in Indonesia were identified, encompassing fields such as communication studies, education, linguistics, computer science, law, and religious studies. However, this number is relatively small compared to the frequency of hate crime cases reported (see Figure 5). While previous studies have established a strong link between hate speech, social media, political factors, and discrimination, the adoption of critical approaches in this area remains minimal. Sirulhaq et al. argued that this limitation stems from a prevailing perception of hate speech in Indonesia as a personal issue rather than an ideological one. As a result, the ideological roots of hate speech have been largely overlooked, posing significant challenges to effectively addressing this phenomenon without a deeper understanding of its underlying causes.

In the field of language in legal processes, scholars have applied pragmatics, discourse analysis, and systemic functional linguistics to analyze language use in police interviews and courtroom settings. The following examples illustrate some of the most prominent approaches used in selected publications.

1) Speech acts

   Purnama (2023) used speech act theory to examine the pragmatic features of verbal attacks in Indonesian courtrooms, drawing data from publicly available transcripts. Other studies have applied speech act analysis to courtroom discourse (e.g. Zulaeha et al., 2022) and police interview (e.g. Firdaus et al., 2019)

2) Presupposition

   Hadiyani (2014) used a presupposition framework in police interviews to uncover the underlying assumptions in investigators' questions.

3) Cooperative principles

   Ramadani et al. (2023) applied Grice's cooperative principles to analyze police interrogations in a theft case in Indonesia. All four maxims – quantity, quality, relevance, and manner – were observed, with avoidance occurring in several exchanges. Similar frameworks have been used in other studies of police interview (e.g. Santoso & Apriyanto, 2020; Satria et al., 2022).

4) Narrative statement analysis

   Kusumanegara et al. (2022) employed Olsson's (2008) narrative statement analysis to examine trial transcripts from three cases in Indonesian Religious Courts, categorizing statements by time, place, sequence, description, and other words.

5) Appraisal theory

   Hermawan et al. (2021) applied Martin and White's appraisal theory (2005) to analyze the plea of an accused in a corruption trial, focusing on evaluative strategies used to counter the prosecution's narrative.

The relatively small number of publications on language and the law indicates that researchers have primarily employed discourse analysis, critical discourse analysis, and argumentative analysis. The following examples present prominent frameworks relevant to the study, with descriptions illustrating their application in selected publications.

1) Text analysis

   Marlia et al. (2023) employed Bivins' (2008) text analysis framework to examine the complexity of Indonesian legal language in the Job Creation Law and propose plain language alternatives.

2) Critical discourse analysis

> Zifana, et al. (2021) applied van Leeuwen's (2004) Critical Discourse Analysis to examine court verdicts in Indonesian defamation cases.

3) Argumentation theory

> Subuki et al. (2023) applied Toulmin's (2003) and Walton's (2006) argumentation theory to examine the reasoning in an Indonesian court verdict imposing the death penalty.

3.2 Methodological Approaches

In forensic linguistics, as in other fields of study, methodology should match the research question, data, and goals. Rigorous and transparent approaches ensure valid and reliable findings, especially for publication in high-ranking journals where clarity and credibility are essential.

Most forensic linguistics research in Indonesia has traditionally relied heavily on qualitative methodologies, often incorporating descriptive statistics to analyze the frequency of linguistic features. However, recent years have witnessed a growing emphasis on interdisciplinary approaches. For instance, corpus linguistics has gained prominence in research on cyberbullying (e.g. Puspitasari, 2022) and hate-speech (e.g. Sirulhaq et al., 2023). Indonesian scholars utilize corpus search systems that are either web-based or software-based (applications), including CQPWeb, AntConc, and LancsBox. These tools facilitate linguistic analysis and enhance the methodological rigor of forensic linguistic research in Indonesia. In addition, several Indonesian language corpora have been available to support forensic linguistics research in the Indonesian context, including: Leipzig Corpora Collection (https://corpora.uni-leipzig.de/en?corpusId=>ind_mixed_2013), language corpus for natural language processing (https://github.com/kmkurn/id-nlp-resource), Korpus Indonesia or Koin (https://korpusindonesia.kemdikbud.go.id/index.php?r=site/about), SEAlang Library Indonesian Text Corpus (https://sealang.net/indonesia/corpus.htm), and abusive Indonesian language training data (https://fold.aston.ac.uk/handle/123456789/30, https://hatespeechdata.com/#Indonesian-header).

Techniques such as N-gram analysis and stylometry have been employed in authorship analysis (e.g. Puspitasari et al., 2024). Furthermore, scholars are increasingly integrating perspectives from fields such as psychology (Bachari et al., 2019; Lubis et al., 2023; Muniroh, 2019; Muniroh & Heydon, 2022), computer science (Puspitasari et al., 2023, e.g. 2024, 2025), and nursing and health (e.g. Muniroh & Heydon, 2024) to achieve a deeper understanding of language use in legal contexts. This cross-disciplinary method enables more nuanced and holistic analyses of forensic linguistic research. Researchers and law enforcement officers used and are introduced to incorporate tools or softwares for language processing such as Lancsbox, ELAN (EUDICO Linguistic Annotator), PRAAT, AntConc, and AntWordProfiler.

3.3 Interdisciplinary Connections and Collaborations

While methodological advancements in forensic linguistics research have integrated insights from other disciplines, authorship patterns often reflect a limited range of contributors: (1) university-based research when research is conducted by academics affiliated with Indonesian universities (e.g. Sinar et al., 2021) and (2) government agency involvement when researchers affiliated with national agencies contributed to the field (e.g. Kusumawardani & Puspitasari, 2021; Sukma et al., 2021). While interuniversity and interinstitutional collaborations exist, they often follow specific patterns. Interuniversity collaborations frequently occur within university networks, often involving collaborations between students, graduates, and their former supervisors (e.g. Hermawan et al., 2021; Sirulhaq et al., 2023; Vidhiasi et al., 2024). Interinstitutional collaborations typically arise from established partnerships between institutions or derive from collegial partnerships (e.g. Muniroh et al., 2022; Puspitasari et al., 2023, 2025). These patterns are not surprising considering the inherent nature of academic collaborations.

International collaborations, while crucial for advancing the field, remain relatively limited. Notable exceptions include the work of Muniroh and Heydon (2022, 2024), Muniroh et al. (2018), and Susanto et al. (2017). These collaborations, often involving former supervisors and their students, demonstrate the potential for Indonesian academics to achieve international recognition, which is increasingly important in the context of the globalizing higher education landscape.

Furthermore, while strong connections between academics and law enforcement agencies are essential for effective forensic linguistics research, these collaborations are still under development in many cases. Currently, collaborations primarily involve law enforcement agencies as research partners, primarily facilitating data collection. However, future collaborations should aim to involve law enforcement agencies more actively in the research process, such as in the co-designing of research questions and the identification of critical research needs. These collaborations will ensure that research findings are highly relevant to real-world legal challenges and contribute significantly to the practical application of forensic linguistics in the justice system.

4 Forensic Linguistic Practices in Indonesia

The role of forensic linguists in developing the field in Indonesia either as insiders/practitioners or as outsiders/researchers are equally important. Shuy (2000) defined insiders or practitioners as those involved in law cases, often producing reports and testimonies, and occasionally testifying in court as expert witnesses. On the other hand, outsiders or researchers are those who are not involved in litigation, but instead study the language of the law, including statutes, trial language, police interviews and witness language. This section discusses the role of practitioners only, while the role of researchers has been discussed in the previous section.

Despite the long-standing contributions of forensic linguists as expert witnesses in Indonesian courts, the profession lacks formal accreditation. While *Badan Bahasa* has been working toward a certification scheme for its own language experts since 2018,[55] a broader accreditation system for forensic linguists has yet to be implemented.

Article 28 Section (1) of the Indonesian Criminal Procedure Code (KUHAP) defines expert testimony as the statement given by a person who possesses special expertise on a matter necessary to clarify a criminal case for the purpose of investigation. Furthermore, Article 184 Section (1) of the KUHAP recognizes expert testimony as one of the valid forms of evidence in criminal proceedings. While KUHAP allows for expert testimony, it does not provide specific criteria for the qualifications of expert witnesses. It states that as long as an individual possesses specialized knowledge relevant to the case and is presented by a party involved in the case, their testimony can be admitted into evidence.

The role of interpreters in legal settings is formally recognized by the Indonesian Criminal Procedure Code (KUHAP). The KUHAP states that defendants or witnesses who do not understand Indonesian have the right to the assistance of an interpreter (Article 53 Section (1) and Article 177). While the KUHAP acknowledges the importance of interpreters, it lacks specific criteria for their qualifications. Courts often require interpreters to present their membership card from the Association of Indonesian Translators (HPI). However, it is crucial to understand that possessing a HPI membership card does not automatically guarantee that an individual is a certified interpreter.

---

[55] https://rumahpusbin.kemdikbud.go.id/datapusbin/7_Pedoman_Sertifikasi_Ahli_Bahasa.pdf, accessed February 3, 2025.

Here, there is a common misconception among some judges that possessing a HPI membership card automatically signifies that an individual is a certified and qualified interpreter.[56] This misconception arises from the assumption that membership in a professional organization guarantees a certain (high) level of expertise.

In contrast to the relatively limited formal recognition for forensic linguists, the field of interpreting has seen some progress with the establishment of professional organizations like HPI. These organizations have developed accreditation schemes and codes of ethics, contributing to the professionalization of the field and ensuring higher standards of quality in interpreting services.

The relatively broad framework of both expert witnesses and interpreters in legal settings highlight the need for clearer guidelines and a more formalized recognition of the profession of forensic linguists in Indonesia. This section addresses the provision of language experts, the writing of affidavit or expert witness report, and standardization and best practices in Indonesia.

4.1 Provision of Language Experts

This section outlines how language experts – such as forensic linguists or interpreters – are engaged in criminal investigation processes and court proceedings. Typically, three main parties request the involvement of language experts: the Indonesian National Police, the Office of the Attorney General of the Republic of Indonesia, and lawyers.

In most cases, language experts are academics, and their testimony can be provided at the investigation stage, the prosecution stage, and/or the court trial stage. Their involvement is not required at every stage of the judicial process; rather, they are consulted when their expertise is deemed necessary.

The police officers often have a list of potential experts to consult as part of standard operating procedures.[57] If they do not have a specific expert in mind, they informally seek recommendations from other academics they know and trust. For instance, the first author was approached by her police colleagues for recommendations on who could assist with a case, and she subsequently referred a suitable expert.

Language experts may be involved with police investigators at different stages of a case. In the pre-investigation stage – before a case is formally

---

[56] https://translationpapersbali.com/2020/10/02/penerjemah-lisan-atau-juru-bahasa-pengadilan/, accessed January 16, 2025.

[57] For example, Standard Operating Procedures for Summoning Experts published by Directorate of Corruption Crimes, Criminal Investigation Agency (Bareskrim), Indonesian National Police (Polri); see https://zi.tipidkorpolri.info/files/SOP-Pemanggilan-Ahli-u2.pdf, accessed February 8, 2025.

pursued and before determination of the status of becoming suspects – language experts may provide an initial opinion that helps investigators assess the strength of the evidence and decide whether to proceed. Their expertise can contribute to the investigators' confidence in the case.

During the investigation stage, where suspects' status has been determined, language experts are interviewed by investigators for their analysis of the linguistic evidence in question, and their responses are documented in *Berita Acara Pemeriksaan* or BAP (ENG police investigation report). For this purpose of investigation, according to the standard procedures, law enforcement agencies send a formal request letter – along with a list of case-related questions – to an institution to obtain a language expert. In response, the institution assigns their language expert to carry out the task. More specifically, when the request is submitted to *Badan Bahasa* or its representative offices across Indonesia, depending on the location of the requesting police, prosecutor, or lawyer's office, the procedure follows these steps.[58]

1) The requestor of service submits a Letter of Request for Language Expert Witness services.
2) The administrator processes the request letter.
3) The leadership appoints a staff member to provide the Language Expert Witness services.
4) The administrator issues an assignment letter for the appointed staff.
5) The appointed staff member coordinates further with the relevant parties.

Language experts may also be involved in later judicial proceedings. Prosecutors' office or lawyers might invite them to provide testimonies before judges in court, particularly when clarifications are needed regarding their opinions in the police investigation report. Supreme Court Decision No. 191 K/Sip/1962 dated October 10, 1962, affirms how many experts need to be heard and states that the assessment of expert and witness testimony is entirely at the discretion of the judge.

Indonesia's linguistic diversity often requires law enforcement to engage interpreters or language experts for ethnic languages. Police requests are usually directed to local *Badan Bahasa* offices, many of which have staff fluent in regional languages, for example, Batak and Nias in North Sumatra, or Sasak and Samawa in West Nusa Tenggara. When in-house expertise is lacking, offices contact language activists, university lecturers in regional languages, or the Indonesian Association of Translators (HPI), drawing on partner contact lists.

---

[58] https://sippn.menpan.go.id/pelayanan-publik/8186309/balai-bahasa-provinsi-aceh/saksi-ahli-bahasa, accessed February 4, 2025.

This system leverages community networks, academic expertise, and professional associations but lacks a centralized pool of trained interpreters for all ethnic languages. Reliance on external partners can cause delays or inconsistent quality, creating potential linguistic disadvantages for speakers of less common languages.

In the analysis of linguistic evidence, a language expert may not only focus on examining the disputed text but could also suggest the possibility of mediation, particularly when the victim and perpetrator share a family relationship. This suggestion remains within the scope of linguistic expertise. Specifically, the language expert may analyze the linguistic data to reveal whether the speaker truly intended to cause harm through language. Drawing on the nature of the speech act (e.g., defamation, misunderstanding, politeness strategies) and sociolinguistic and cultural insights, the expert may identify relational dynamics, such as family ties or social hierarchies – that suggests the case could be more constructively resolved outside formal prosecution. From this analysis, the expert may conclude that while the utterance was harmful, the cultural context especially in settings that highly value social harmony supports restorative approaches such as mediation. The actual mediation, however, is conducted by police officers, trained mediators, or other neutral parties – not by the linguist.

An example of this is found in Inderasari et al. (2022) in a defamation case involving an uncle and a nephew with a Javanese cultural background. In this case, the nephew posted on social media about his uncle's behavior, which he considered inappropriate and insulting. The uncle got offended, feeling that his nephew had defamed him. Believing his nephew had crossed the line, he reported the case to the police. Following the language expert's suggestion, the police facilitated mediation between the two parties. The police encouraged the nephew, as the younger person, to take the initiative to apologize to his uncle, as this aligns with the Javanese tradition of respecting elders. Ultimately, the conflict was resolved through mediation.

4.2 Writing Expert Reports

When reporting the results of a linguistic evidence analysis, a language expert may prepare an expert report. While writing an expert report is not currently mandatory, law enforcement officers highly appreciate experts who provide this important document, as it comprehensively presents the expert's opinions on matters within their expertise. This section outlines the key elements of an expert report and the approach to analyzing a case.

Table 3 Components in linguistic expert testimony reports

No	Components	Description
1.	Cover page	The cover page should include the following components: – Title – Clearly indicating the nature of the report and the specific case or analysis the expert was instructed to conduct. – Reference Number – As stated in the letter of request from law enforcement. – Addressee/Requestor – The authority or institution to whom the report is submitted. – Source of Instruction – The individual or organization that requested the expert analysis. – Subject Matter of Analysis – A brief description of the linguistic evidence or issue under examination. – Date of Report – The date when the expert report was produced. – Expert Signature – Including the expert's full name, academic/professional titles, affiliated institution, institution's address, and the expert's contact details (email and phone number).
2.	Introduction	This section provides context for the case in which linguistic evidence is being analyzed. It also offers a preview of the report's contents and structure.
3.	Instructions	This section outlines the scope of the inquiry and lists the specific questions the expert has been asked to address. The expert may directly quote the instructions as stated in the letter of request.
4.	Subject Matter of Analysis	This section details the documents, texts, or files received from law enforcement for analysis.
5.	Expert Qualification	A summary paragraph explaining the relevance of the expert's qualifications and expertise to the case. More detailed information can be provided in an attached CV.
6.	Theoretical Framework	An explanation of the linguistic principles, theoretical framework, or methodology that the expert will use for the analysis.

Table 3 (cont.)

No	Components	Description
7.	Results	The expert's responses to the questions outlined in the instructions, presented in the same order for clarity and coherence.
8.	Conclusion	A summary of the expert's professional opinions on the case based on the analysis.
9.	Statement of Truth	A declaration that the expert recognizes their overriding duty to the court and has complied with this duty in providing the report.
10.	Signature	The expert's full name, date, and signature.
11.	References	This section provides a list of all references cited in the report, following a consistent citation style (e.g., APA, MLA, or any format specified by the requesting authority).

Based on our experience in preparing expert reports, the following components should be included.

When preparing an expert report, the expert should follow a structured approach similar to conducting research. The following key considerations should be ensured when analyzing linguistic evidence (see Kusno, 2021).

4.3 Model of Analysis and Ethics

This section addresses two key aspects: (1) a model for analyzing cases involving disputed meanings, where a language expert is tasked with determining whether the utterances or texts in question constitute defamation, insult, hate speech, or other forms of language conflict or language war, and (2) the ethical principles that language experts must adhere to in the course of their work.

In this context, "language war" refers to the deliberate use of language as a tool or weapon by a speaker or writer to advance their own interests or those of their group. The purpose is to attack the ideas, thoughts, behavior, honor, or physical condition of an individual or a group of interlocutors, either directly or indirectly (Aziz, 2020). Language war can be categorized along a continuum based on the level of harm inflicted on the victim. The continuum starts with suggestion, which has the least impact or potential of losing face, and progresses toward slander, which has the most significant effect. In between, the sequence unfolds as criticism, mockery, incitement, defamation, and insult, each

Table 4 Key considerations in the analysis of linguistic evidence

No.	Consideration	Description
1.	Clearly define key terms	Formulate operational definitions relevant to the case, such as defining hate speech or other legal and linguistic concepts.
2.	Enhance contextual understanding	Where possible, consult with police investigators to gather supporting information from witnesses or suspects.
3.	Collect relevant data for triangulation	Supplement findings with information from other sources, such as media reports or precedent cases with permanent legal force.
4.	Select appropriate theories and methodologies	Base the analysis on established theoretical frameworks and methodologies informed by previous research in similar investigations.
5.	Exercise caution in analysis and conclusions	Maintain a careful and objective approach when analyzing linguistic data as legal evidence, as the findings may significantly impact an individual's rights and livelihood.

increasing in intensity. The severity of a language war can escalate based on how the target is referenced or identified, as outlined by Aziz (2020). At one end of the continuum, an implicit reference without specific identification leaves room for debate on potential criminal liability; clarity of the identity of the suspect is subtlety hidden. At the other end, an explicit mention of the target removes any doubt about liability, making the potential suspect obvious to the public. Between these two extremes, the level of liability increases with the following types of references:

– Mentioning of initials
– Describing general characteristics of a reference
– Describing specific characteristics of a reference

The model for analysis involves three main considerations, namely (1) utterance as the focal point of analysis, (2) holisticism of analysis, and (3) speech acts as theoretical bases for analytical framework.

1) Utterance as the focal point of analysis

The primary focus of analysis is on the utterances in question. The utterances will appear with various accompanying features, which at a minimum will represent Speaker, Hearer, and Context. Context refers to the setting of the utterance (time, place, prosody), the topic of the utterance, and the textual environment.

The term "utterance" is used here to contrast its concept with sentence as defined in the study of Syntax. While most of the data analyzed are spoken, written data are also included, provided they are treated as representations of spoken utterances. We define utterance as any stretch of talk performed in a given context bounded by silence before and after its articulation. When written, an utterance may consist of a sequence of sentences, or a single phrase, or even a single word. Each utterance is believed to contain a proposition.

2) Holisticism of analysis

This entails systematic analyses of all elements of the utterance, which can be parsed into as small as morphophonemic elements or into as big as a set of complete textual discourse. Analysis can also involve the search of paralinguistic concomitants that can influence the interpretation of linguistic phenomena. This holistic approach ensures accuracy and reliability in the analysis.

3) Speech acts as the theoretical bases for analytical framework

The analysis is guided by speech act theories, which will examine the intended meaning, function, and impact of the utterances within their social and cultural context.

The utterance is analyzed according to its class, that is, constatives or performatives. Constatives are analyzed in terms of the truth conditions (whether the statement can be judged true or false). Performatives, on the other hand, are analyzed in terms of felicity conditions (whether the utterance is appropriate and effective within its context). Felicity conditions involve three key aspects (cf. Allan, 1986; Bach & Harnish, 1979; Searle, 1969):

– The preparatory conditions (P) refer to the readiness requirement, the appropriateness of speech, and the absolute authority of a speaker to perform or not perform an action.
– The sincerity conditions (S) refer to the speaker's genuine intention for an utterance to occur or not occur, which demands honesty and deliberateness in producing the utterance.

– The illocutionary intention (I) refers to the intended purpose of an utterance. It clarifies the essential goal of the speech act. For example, an utterance may serve as an accusation, confession, promise, command, etc.

It is evident from the previous sections that there is currently no certification for forensic linguists, and the association still requires support to sustain its activities. Therefore, considering its vital role, scholars like Aziz have formulated the following ethical principles that language experts must adhere to (Aziz, 2020).

1) Honesty

Stating the truth as it is, in accordance with the factual data available and the knowledge and understanding possessed.

2) Fairness

Being impartial towards the parties involved in the case.

3) Professionalism

Providing opinions in accordance with the scientific principles they possess or understand, as a form of professional responsibility in upholding the essence and dignity of truth.

4) Proportionality

Not judgmental but limited to offering guidance for parties involved in the judicial process. This guidance remains firmly within the scope of linguistics, for example, by clarifying ambiguities, identifying inconsistencies in language use, and interpreting meaning based on linguistic principles.

5) Credibility

Capable of maintaining the confidentiality of data and the identities of the parties involved in the case until it is declared open to the public by a judge's ruling.

5 Conclusion and Final Thought

The development of forensic linguistics in Indonesia, from its early milestones to its progress up to 2024, reflects more positive advancements than major obstacles. While its growth has been gradual, the need for forensic linguistics in the legal system is evident, the gap between research, practice and policy development remains clear, and the interest from academics and institutions continues to grow – highlighting its significance and future potential. This section summarizes the key discussions, presents challenges, and outlines the future directions for the field.

5.1 Summary

In this Element, forensic linguistics is defined as the interdisciplinary scientific study of language applied in legal and investigative settings. It covers various areas, including the analysis of linguistic evidence, the examination of spoken and written legal communication, the interpretation of legal documents, and the promotion of forensic linguistic literacy. The ultimate goal is to contribute to fairer justice processes. To explore the origins, progress, and future directions of forensic linguistics in Indonesia, this Element integrates survey data from academics and practitioners alongside a systematic literature search conducted using *Publish or Perish* software.

The Element discusses the development of forensic linguistics in Indonesia, which has progressed from public criticism of authorities to the formal inclusion of linguists in legal proceedings, as mandated by regulations. The origins of forensic linguistics in Indonesia can be traced back to early language-related cases during the Soekarno or Old Order era, the first academic contribution to a judicial process in 1995, and the initial scholarly publication in the media that same year. The term "forensic linguistics" was first mentioned in Indonesian media in 2002, marking a significant step in the field's recognition and development (see Figure 3).

In its early stages, the growth of forensic linguistics in Indonesia was largely driven by academics who were introduced to the field during their master's or doctoral studies abroad. This exposure played a crucial role in disseminating and expanding the discipline, sparking research in areas such as disputed meaning, police interviews, courtroom discourse, and legal interpretation. Over time, the field has continued to evolve, with linguists employing diverse theories and concepts, methodological approaches, integrating interdisciplinary perspectives, and fostering collaborations – both with international scholars for research and publication and with legal professionals for capacity building and language awareness initiatives.

Underlying these advancements, forensic linguistics in Indonesia exhibits three key characteristics. First, many scholars in the field come from diverse linguistic backgrounds, developing their expertise through research, practical experience, and specialized training rather than formal master's or doctoral programs in forensic linguistics. Second, the role of language as evidence has become increasingly prominent, largely driven by the growing needs of the justice sector. Lastly, linguists have gained authoritative recognition, contributing to the expansion and credibility of forensic linguistics in Indonesia.

Support for forensic linguistics has extended beyond higher education institutions, where the field has been integrated into bachelor's, master's, and doctoral programs through 2–6 credit hour courses. Non-higher education institutions have also acknowledged its significance, promoting engagement through expert collaborations and knowledge-sharing initiatives. The number of language experts – both forensic linguists and interpreters – offering testimony in language-related cases and facilitating communication in judicial processes has steadily grown, including specialists in local languages. Their expertise is increasingly sought not only by the Indonesian National Police and the Office of the Attorney General but also by lawyers, with forensic linguists playing a role at various stages of judicial proceedings.

Efforts to strengthen capacity building in forensic linguistics have been largely incidental, supported through workshops, seminars, and masterclasses organized by universities and government institutions. These training programs cater not only to professionals, such as linguists seeking to refine their skills in language analysis and law enforcement officers aiming to enhance their language awareness, but also to the general public. By educating laypeople on the responsible use of language, these initiatives help prevent individuals from becoming involved in language-related crimes. This broader approach reflects the growing efforts to integrate forensic linguistics into the legal system and enhance its recognition by law enforcement agencies. As a result, such initiatives have reinforced the role of forensic linguistics in legal proceedings, further solidifying its importance in ensuring linguistic expertise within judicial processes.

5.2 Challenges

Forensic linguistics has undeniably reached a level of maturity in the world globally, as demonstrated by its institutional recognition, theoretical foundations, methodological advancements, professional practice, ethical standards, and legal impact. This assessment is based on benchmarking against developments in developed countries such as the UK, particularly as represented by the Aston Institute for Forensic Linguistics. In this context, forensic linguistics has evolved into a dynamic research discipline, supported by institutional structures, methodologies, and academic cultures that actively foster new knowledge, critical inquiry, and theoretical advancements. Forensic linguistics in Indonesia can be further established, considering its current stage of development. Achieving this requires outlining and addressing challenges to strengthen its foundation.

Establishing forensic linguistics in Indonesia remains a complex endeavor due to the country's vast linguistic diversity, which includes numerous languages, dialects, and ethnic groups. This diversity demands extensive documentation and poses challenges for directly applying forensic linguistic methods developed for English or other major languages to Indonesian and its local languages. Muniroh's adaptation of cognitive interviewing highlights these difficulties (Muniroh, 2019). Translating phrases like "think of" and "get a clear picture in your mind" was challenging (see also Lai, 2016), as was finding an appropriate equivalent for "you" due to Indonesian's open referencing system (Muniroh & Heydon, 2024). These issues become even more pronounced when considering local languages, as information retrieval is often more effective in the language where events are originally encoded in memory (Filipović, 2011). Additionally, regional variations in dialect, accent, and speech patterns complicate linguistic analysis on language evidence, linguistic profiling and authorship analysis, particularly when experts lack familiarity with these linguistic nuances. As we can see in Section 4.1, various ethnic language interpreters and experts were in fact available through the representative offices of Badan Bahasa across Indonesia, but the number of experts is lower than that of the number of languages in Indonesia, that is, 718 languages, 778 dialects, and 43 subdialects as detailed in Section 1.3.3. Furthermore, there is a pressing need for tools or technologies that can be directly utilized for forensic linguistic analysis, such as authorship analysis, with relatively high accuracy and reliability.

Regarding ethnic diversity, it is crucial to adopt problem-solving approaches that are sensitive to ethnic norms and values, as illustrated in Section 4.1. This sensitivity presents an opportunity for forensic linguists to explore the possibility of mediation in language-related crimes involving individuals of the same ethnicity. However, a challenge lies in ensuring that such mediation processes remain impartial and do not inadvertently reinforce existing power imbalances within or between ethnic groups. Ethnic identity can influence communication styles, perceptions of authority, and expectations regarding justice, all of which may affect both the mediation process and its outcomes.

Ethnicity-related issues can also introduce concerns such as ethnic bias in judicial decision-making (cf. Choi et al., 2022). While there is no documented evidence of this occurring in Indonesia, recognizing ethnicity as a potential source of judicial bias is essential for ensuring due process. In-group favoritism can lead to coethnic bias, where judges may be more inclined to grant appeals from individuals of their own ethnicity over those from different ethnic backgrounds. To the best of the authors' knowledge, judges assigned to a particular region may come from different ethnic backgrounds than the majority population in that area. For instance, at the West Java District Court, judges are not only of Sundanese ethnicity but also from other ethnic groups such as Batak, Minang, and Bugis.

Another challenge concerns institutional and legal recognition. While forensic linguistics has gained significant traction in Indonesia in recent years and has been utilized by legal institutions, as discussed in Section 2.1.2, many law enforcement officers, prosecutors, and judges still have limited awareness of the field and its practical applications. Compared to forensic disciplines such as medical forensics, digital forensics, and forensic psychology, forensic linguistics remains less widely recognized. Notably, the online version of *Kamus Besar Bahasa Indonesia* (ENG the Great Dictionary of the Indonesian Language) still defines "forensik" primarily in relation to medical forensics, although the term "forensik" has already been included after the entry *linguistik* (ENG linguistics). Furthermore, forensic linguistic research in Indonesia tends to be more descriptive, with limited influence on policy development. The field also continues to face challenges in achieving universal recognition as an expert domain within the legal community.

Lastly, a significant challenge lies in educational and training gaps. While linguistics is widely taught in Indonesian universities, as discussed in Section 2.1.1, forensic linguistics remains a course rather than a full-fledged study program. Establishing such a program requires careful consideration of professional and career pathways, which remain unclear in Indonesia. Unlike translators or interpreters, forensic linguists are not yet widely recognized as a distinct profession, making it difficult for graduates to secure employment outside academia. Moreover, as highlighted in Section 4.1, there is a lack of standardized competency frameworks for forensic analysts as well as a systematic workshop or training program for becoming a forensic linguist. Currently, forensic linguists in Indonesia typically hold established roles as lecturers or language specialists, such as those in *Badan Bahasa*.

5.3 Future Directions

Challenges should be seen as opportunities for improvement, informing future directions to strengthen and sustain growth of forensic linguistics in Indonesia. A multipronged approach is essential to achieving this goal.

While Indonesia's linguistic and cultural diversity is one of its defining characteristics, it should be managed in a way that contributes to the advancement of forensic linguistic analysis. Addressing this and other related challenges requires a comprehensive approach that includes conducting research that embraces linguistic diversity, standardizing forensic linguistic practices, strengthening or revitalizing professional associations and research centers, and promoting research that informs policy development.

Documenting linguistic diversity through the creation of linguistic databases plays a crucial role in enhancing forensic linguistic analysis. Developing corpora of legal and forensic language data, while examining lexical and syntactic variations across languages and dialects, can significantly improve analytical accuracy. For example, language-related crimes such as hate speech and insults often involve swear words; building a specialized corpus of these linguistic elements can aid forensic analysis and contribute to the development of a hate speech database. These databases can also serve as valuable resources for training, research, and reference in forensic linguistics.

To maximize effectiveness, linguists should invest in forensic linguistic technology that accommodates Indonesia's diverse languages and dialects – a need that has been emphasized in the preceding discussion. For instance, in a case involving hate speech on social media, a forensic linguist could utilize a specialized language model trained on hate speech corpora across multiple Indonesian dialects. Such a system would enable the identification of offensive language patterns, flag implicit threats, and provide contextual analysis to support legal proceedings.

Furthermore, forensic linguists should develop expertise in multiple regional languages and dialects while collaborating with sociolinguists, anthropologists, and legal experts. This interdisciplinary approach ensures a deeper understanding of how language and culture intersect with forensic analysis, ultimately strengthening forensic linguistic practices in Indonesia.

Standardization is essential in forensic linguistics, particularly in legal processes and the assessment of linguistic evidence. However, it must be applied in a way that acknowledges linguistic diversity rather than disregarding it. Globally, police investigations have shifted from traditional interrogation methods to science-based approaches, with investigative interviewing becoming widely recommended. When adapting and implementing investigative interviewing within the Indonesian policing context, it is crucial to consider not only linguistic factors but also regional languages and sociocultural norms. These elements should be integrated into relevant stages of interviewing, while ensuring that the final reports are presented in Indonesian. This approach enables police officers across Indonesia to conduct interviews effectively using a standardized method while maintaining sensitivity to local linguistic and cultural contexts.

To achieve this balance, forensic linguistic protocols must be designed to account for language variation while maintaining legal and scientific rigor. This approach not only ensures consistency in forensic linguistic practices but also allows for necessary adaptations that reflect Indonesia's complex linguistic and cultural landscape. In line with standardization, to effectively implement these strategies, forensic linguistics training programs should be designed to address specific linguistic and cultural contexts within Indonesia. Such training can help legal professionals and forensic linguists apply forensic linguistic principles effectively while respecting the nation's linguistic diversity.

Technology can also play a crucial role in standardizing forensic work, particularly in addressing issues such as ethnic bias in judicial decisions. Research on the use of Artificial Intelligence (AI) in forensic linguistics has shown promising results in mitigating bias and improving consistency in forensic analysis (e.g. Lopes, 2024; Rosili et al., 2020).

Another challenge concerns institutional and legal recognition. Addressing this issue requires a strategic and collaborative effort between forensic linguists and law enforcement agencies. Collaborating with law enforcement officers offers various opportunities to integrate their expertise into forensic linguistics. One approach is to invite them as speakers at forensic linguistics conferences or seminars, a practice that has already been implemented, recognizing their valuable perspectives on enhancing the delivery of justice. Similarly, conducting community service programs for law enforcement by academics, such as training on language evidence analysis, police interviewing, or the role of interpreters in legal settings, has also been practiced, further strengthening engagement between forensic linguists and the legal community. Beyond these efforts, working together on ethics committees when research involves individuals within the judicial process can foster ethical oversight and mutual understanding. Such partnerships can ultimately enhance effective advocacy and promote the practical application of forensic linguistics in legal contexts.

Strengthening or revitalizing professional organizations and research centers on forensic linguistics within universities is essential. By working collectively with a shared vision and clear objectives, these organizations can take a more structured, systematic, and professional approach to enhancing recognition in the field. Additionally, they can serve as catalysts for the establishment and growth of forensic linguistics in Indonesia by developing capacity-building training programs, setting professional standards, raising language awareness among legal professionals and the public, and securing institutional support. Moreover, such initiatives will help bridge educational and training gaps by creating well-defined pathways for professional development in forensic linguistics.

More specifically, as outlined in Section 3, forensic linguistics research in Indonesia primarily focuses on language as evidence, with limited exploration of language in legal processes and language and the law. However, there are many emerging and underexplored areas such as indigenous language-related cases where forensic linguists can expand their research beyond descriptive analysis to actively contribute to policy recommendations. One of the key research-related challenges is ensuring that forensic linguistic studies have practical implications for legal and institutional reforms. Encouraging collaborative research with law enforcement agencies and jointly identifying research problems can enhance the likelihood of influencing policy and legal practices. While this approach presents challenges – not only for forensic linguistics as an emerging field in Indonesia but also for other disciplines – it offers a strategic pathway for integrating linguistic insights into legal and institutional frameworks, ultimately strengthening the role of forensic linguistics in shaping policy development. Additionally, increasing publication efforts in both national and international journals is essential to enhance Indonesia's contribution to the global forensic linguistics discourse.

These future directions would help clarify career pathways for forensic linguists and contribute to the advancement of forensic linguistics in Indonesia, ensuring its broader recognition and impact within legal and academic domains.

References

Abdullah, I., Jubba, H., Pabbajah, M. et al. (2019). From selfism to indifferentism: Challenges facing Indonesian society and culture, 2015–2045. *Academic Journal of Interdisciplinary Studies*, 8, 102–112. https://doi.org/10.36941/ajis-2019-0009.

Abubakar, A., & Din, M. (2022). Bahasa hukum Qanun Jinayat Aceh: Teks lama untuk konteks baru. *Legitimasi: Jurnal Hukum Pidana Dan Politik Hukum*, 11(1), 1. https://doi.org/10.22373/legitimasi.v11i1.13450.

Adbaka, F., & Datang, F. A. (2023). Forensic linguistic analysis: Civil servant speech equating prostitutes with Probolinggo parliament members. *Lingua Cultura*, 17(2), 253–260. https://doi.org/10.21512/lc.v17i2.10645.

Adi, Y. A., & Bahri, M. T. (2023). Conflict and perspectives: The social construction of Chinese ethnic citizens against natives in Surakarta, Indonesia after the May 1998 Riots. *RESIPROKAL: Jurnal Riset Sosiologi Progresif Aktual*, 5(1), 15–30. https://doi.org/10.29303/resiprokal.v5i1.278.

Ainsworth, J. (2021). How I got started. *Language and Law/Linguagem e Direito*, 7(1–2), 30–32. https://ojs.letras.up.pt/index.php/LLLD/article/view/10347.

Alduais, A., Al-Khulaidi, M. A., Allegretta, S., & Abdulkhalek, M. M. (2023). Forensic linguistics: A scientometric review. *Cogent Arts and Humanities*, 10 (1). https://doi.org/10.1080/23311983.2023.2214387.

Allan, K. (1986). *Linguistic meaning* (Vol. 1). Routledge & Kegan Paul.

Amani, H. Z., Indrayani, S., & Sofa, N. (2023). Equivalent of archaic words in modern English: A study on the translation of laws and regulations of the Republic of Indonesia. *LinguAmerta: Linguistics, Literature and Translation Studies*, 1(1), 1–17. https://jurnal.pnj.ac.id/index.php/linguamerta/article/view/6408/3326.

Amarini, I., Saefudin, Y., Kartini, I. A., Marsitiningsih, M., & Ismail, N. (2023). Digital transformation: Creating an effective and efficient court in Indonesia. *Legality: Jurnal Ilmiah Hukum*, 2(31), 266–284. https://doi.org/10.22219/ljih.v31i2.28013.

Amin, K. F., & Burhanuddin. (2021). Disclosure of the meaning of sentences in a discourse in the media online as an alleged defamation case: Forensic linguistic studies. *Multicultural Education*, 7(4), 180–185. http://ijdri.com/me/wp-content/uploads/2021/04/21.pdf.

Ana, I. W. (2018). The challenge of the interpreter in interpreting non-native English speakers: A case study – EIT case at Court of Gianyar – Bali. *2nd English Language and Literature International Conference (ELLiC) Proceedings*, 2, 502–509. https://jurnal.unimus.ac.id/index.php/ELLIC/article/view/3580.

Ana, I. W. (2020). The characteristics of Indonesian legal language in notarial documents. *International Linguistics Research*, 3(3), 1. https://doi.org/10.30560/ilr.v3n3p1.

Anisah, A., & Sari, D. F. (2024). The force of questioning and pragmatic strategies in courtroom interrogation: A conversation analysis. *Studies in English Language and Education*, 11(2), 1030–1045. https://doi.org/10.24815/siele.v11i2.35587.

Antara, I. G. N. (2023). A case of defamation: Linguistic forensics study. *The International Journal of Social Sciences World*, 5(1), 93–100.

Ariani, M. G., Sajedi, F., & Sajedi, M. (2014). Forensic linguistics: A brief overview of the key elements. *Procedia – Social and Behavioral Sciences*, 158, 222–225. https://doi.org/10.1016/j.sbspro.2014.12.078.

Arianto, A. K. (2021). Dugaan hoaks seputar vaksin covid-19 di Indonesia dalam kerangka linguistik forensik. *Prosiding Seminar Nasional: Arah Kebijakan Pendidikan Dan Kajian Riset Di Era New Normal*, 3(1), 115–129. https://ejurnal.mercubuana-yogya.ac.id/index.php/Prosiding_KoPeN/article/view/1660.

Arifin, M. (2020). A decade review of civil law in Indonesia. *International Journal of Innovative Research and Advanced Studies (IJIRAS)*, 7(4), 78–83.

Asplund, K. D. (2019, March 23). *Investigative interviewing is taking root in Indonesia*. Norwegian Centre for Human Rights, University of Oslo; Norwegian Centre for Human Rights. www.jus.uio.no/smr/english/about/id/news/ii_kurs_manado2019.html.

Azeez, M. Y. (2024, April). *"The sound of the police" and the readdressing of its role: A comparison of the Indonesian, Sri Lankan, and Cambodian contexts*. Institute for Criminal Justice Reform.

Azis, M. A. (2022). Riset aksi peningkatan kemampuan linguistik forensik bagi penyidik Polri. *Jurnal Litbang Polri*, 25(2), 71–83. https://doi.org/10.46976/.v25i2.186.

Aziz, E. (2024, August 11–16). Language policy and planning in Indonesia: Local language preservation policy and national language globalization initiatives [Conference Presentation]. In *21st AILA World Congress 2024*, Kuala Lumpur Convention Centre, Malaysia.

Aziz, E. A. (2012, March 18). Peran linguistik forensik. *Pikiran Rakyat*.

Aziz, E. A. (2016, February 10). Linguistik forensik. *Pikiran Rakyat*, 26.

Aziz, E. A. (2020). *Analisis linguistik forensik untuk penegakan keadilan.*

Aziz, E. A., & Lukmana, I. (2013). *Merekonstruksi bahasa hukum: Studi kasus teks sumpah jabatan pegawai negeri sipil.*

Aziz, E. A., Muniroh, R. D. D., & Hermawan, R. (2013). *BAP polisi vs pernyataan tersangka: Analisis realisasi linguistik dalam penyidikan perkara pidana dan implikasi hukumnya.*

Aziz, E. A., Muniroh, R. D. D., & Hermawan, R. (2014). *Strategi pengungkapan fakta hukum di pengadilan: Studi tentang strategi bertanya para hakim, jaksa penuntut umum dan penasihat hukum dalam menemukan fakta-fakta dari terperiksa.*

Bach, K., & Harnish, R. M. (1979). *Linguistic communication and speech acts.* The MIT Press.

Bachari, A. D. (2019). Analysis of form and theme of hate speech against President Joko Widodo on social media: A forensic linguistic study. *Proceedings of the Second Conference on Language, Literature, Education, and Culture (ICOLLITE 2018).* https://doi.org/10.2991/icollite-18.2019.49.

Bachari, A. D., Sudana, D., & Gunawan, W. (2019). Ragam dan arah pertanyaan penyidik dalam Berita Acara Pemeriksaan perkara pidana anak. *Linguistik Indonesia,* 36(1), 66–92. https://doi.org/10.26499/li.v36i1.73.

Badan Pengembangan dan Pembinaan Bahasa. (2015, August 28). *Forum diskusi tenaga ahli bahasa di kepolisian dan DPR.* https://Badanbahasa .Kemdikbud.Go.Id/. https://badanbahasa.kemdikbud.go.id/kegiatan-detail/ 1804/forum-diskusi-tenaga-ahli-bahasa-di-kepolisian-dan-dpr.

Badan Pengembangan dan Pembinaan Bahasa. (2016). *Ashadi Siregar (1945 – . . .).* Ensiklopedia Sastra Indonesia. https://ensiklopedia.kemdik bud.go.id/sastra/artikel/Ashadi_Siregar.

Bakker, L. (2023). Custom and violence in Indonesia's protracted land conflict. *Social Sciences & Humanities Open,* 8(1), 100624. https://doi.org/10.1016/j .ssaho.2023.100624.

Batubara, L. (2009, June 19). *Prita korban pertama UU ITE.* Dewan Pers. https:// dewanpers.or.id/publikasi/opini_detail/16/Prita_Korban_Pertama_UU_ITE.

Berk-Seligson, S. (2012). *The bilingual courtroom: Court interpreters in the judicial process.* University of Chicago Press.

Bivins, Peggy Gale. (2008). *Implementing plain language into legal documents: The technical communicator's role.* Orlando: University of Central Florida MA thesis.

Budianto, A., Rato, D., Anggono, B. D., & Setyawan, F. (2022). Restorative justice: Positivization of customary law in resolving land disputes based on local wisdom of Papuan citizens. *Journal of Law, Policy and Globalization,* 127, 1–10.

Budiono, A., Yuspin, W., Nurani, S. S. et al. (2023). The Anglo-Saxon system of common law and the development of the legal system in Indonesia. *WSEAS Transactions on System*, 22, 207–213. https://doi.org/10.37394/23202.2023.22.21.

Butt, S. (2023). Indonesia's new Criminal Code: Indigenising and democratising Indonesian criminal law? *Griffith Law Review*, 32(2), 190–214. https://doi.org/10.1080/10383441.2023.2243772.

Butt, S., & Lindsey, T. (2018). *Indonesian law* (Vol. 1). Oxford University Press. https://doi.org/10.1093/oso/9780199677740.001.0001.

Butt, S., & Lindsey, T. (2020). The Criminal Procedure Code. In T. Lindsey & H. Pausacker (Eds.), *Crime and punishment in Indonesia* (pp. 44–69). Routledge.

Butt, S., & Nathaniel, A. (2024). Evidence from criminal law experts in Indonesian criminal trials: Usurping the judicial function? *The International Journal of Evidence & Proof*, 28(2), 129–153. https://doi.org/10.1177/13657127231217319.

Cammack, M. E., & Feener, R. M. (2012). The Islamic legal system in Indonesia. *Pacific Rim Law & Policy Journal*, 21(13), 13–42. https://digital commons.law.uw.edu/wilj/vol21/iss1/5.

Cheng, L., & Danesi, M. (2019). Exploring legal discourse: a sociosemiotic (re) construction. *Social Semiotics*, 29(3), 279–285. https://doi.org/10.1080/10350330.2019.1587841.

Choi, D. D., Harris, J. A., & Shen-Bayh, F. (2022). Ethnic bias in judicial decision making: Evidence from criminal appeals in Kenya. *American Political Science Review*, 116(3), 1067–1080. https://doi.org/10.1017/S000305542100143X.

Coulthard, M. (2021). A chance encounter. *Language and Law/Linguagem e Direito*, 7(1–2), 33–35. https://ojs.letras.up.pt/index.php/LLLD/article/view/10348.

Coulthard, M., & Johnson, A. (2010). *The Routledge handbook of forensic linguistics*. Routledge. https://doi.org/10.4324/9780203855607.

Coulthard, M., May, A., & Sousa-Silva, R. (2021). *The Routledge handbook of forensic linguistics* (2nd). Routledge.

Coulthard, M., & Sousa-Silva, R. (2021). Editors' introduction. *Language and Law/Linguagem e Direito*, 7(1–2), 1–3. https://ojs.letras.up.pt/index.php/LLLD/article/view/10338.

Crouch, M. (2019). *The politics of court reform: Judicial change and legal culture in Indonesia*. Cambridge University Press. https://doi.org/10.1017/9781108636131.

Crouch, M. (2021). The challenges for court reform after authoritarian rule: The role of specialized courts in Indonesia. *Constitutional Review*, 7(1), 1. https://doi.org/10.31078/consrev711.

Deliana, E., & Rauf, M. A. (2022). Settlement of husband-wife affairs case according to customary law in Mempura district, Siak Sri Indrapura regency. *Social Values & Society*, 4(1), 3–7. https://doi.org/10.26480/svs.01.2022.03.07.

Dewan Perwakilan Rakyat RI. (2021). *Risalah rapat timus pembahasan RUU tentang pembentukan Pengadilan Tinggi Kepulauan Riau, Pengadilan Tinggi Sulawesi Barat, Pengadilan Tinggi Kalimantan Utara, dan Pengadilan Tinggi Papua Barat*. https://berkas.dpr.go.id/akd/dokumen/BALEG-23-2048e3ea71b0c19644ca23edb7ed2f95.pdf.

Dewantara, J. A., Budimansyah, D., Darmawan, C. et al. (2024). Language, cultural sentiments, and ethnic conflict: Understanding verbal violence and discrimination in multi-ethnic schools in West Kalimantan, Indonesia. *Journal of Language, Identity & Education*, 1–17. https://doi.org/10.1080/15348458.2024.2408451.

Dharmaraj, S. (2024, November 19). *Indonesia: AI and digital tools in forensic linguistics*. Open Gov Asia. https://opengovasia.com/2024/11/19/indonesia-ai-and-digital-tools-in-forensic-linguistics/.

Eades, D. (1994). A case of communicative clash: Aboriginal English and the legal system. In J. P. Gibbons (Ed.), *Language and the Law*, (pp. 234–264). London: Routledge.

Eades, D. (2021). How I got started. *Language and Law/Linguagem e Direito*, 7 (1–2), 30–32. https://ojs.letras.up.pt/index.php/LLLD/article/view/10342.

Eades, D., & Pavlenko, A. (2016). Translating research into policy: New guidelines for communicating rights to non-native speakers. *Language and Law/Linguagem e Direito*, 3(2), 45–64. http://aleph.letras.up.pt/index.php/LLLD/article/viewFile/1752/1597.

Faisal, Y. A., Rahayu, D. P., Haryadi, D., Darmawan, A., & Manik, J. D. N. (2024). Genuine paradigm of criminal justice: Rethinking penal reform within Indonesia New Criminal Code. *Cogent Social Sciences*, 10(1), 1–17. https://doi.org/10.1080/23311886.2023.2301634.

Filipović, L. (2011). Speaking and remembering in one or two languages: Bilingual vs. monolingual lexicalization and memory for motion events. *International Journal of Bilingualism*, 15(4), 466–485. https://doi.org/10.1177/1367006911403062.

Finegan, E. (2021). My thwarted start as a forensic linguist. *Language and Law/Linguagem e Direito*, 7(1–2), 20–23. https://ojs.letras.up.pt/index.php/LLLD/article/view/10344.

Firdaus, A. Y., Amelia, F., & Lailiyah, S. (2019). Illocutionary acts and their relationships with interviewees' level of trustworthiness in giving Information during the making of investigation reports: A case study in Situbondo police station. *International Journal of Humanity Studies*, 2(2), 158–166.

Fitzpatrick, D. (1999). Culture, ideology and human rights: The case of Indonesia's Code of Criminal Procedure. In T. Lindsey (Ed.) *Indonesia: Law and Society*, Federation Press. (pp. 499–514).

Fitzpatrick, D. (2007). Land, custom, and the state in post-Suharto Indonesia: A foreign lawyer's perspective. In J. S. Davidson & D. Henley (Eds.), *The revival of tradition in Indonesian politics: The deployment of adat from colonialism to indigenism* (pp. 150–168). Routledge.

Florey, M., & Himmelmann, N. (2010). New directions in field linguistics: Training strategies for language documentation in Indonesia. In M. Florey (Ed.), *Endangered languages of Austronesia* (pp. 121–140). Oxford University Press.

Gibbons, J. (1999). Language and the law. *Annual Review of Applied Linguistics*, 19, 156–173. https://doi.org/10.1017/S0267190599190081.

Gibbons, J. (2021). My first case. *Language and Law/Linguagem e Direito*, 7 (1–2), 28–29. https://ojs.letras.up.pt/index.php/LLLD/article/view/10346.

Grant, T., & MacLeod, N. (2020). *Language and online identities: The undercover policing of internet sexual crime*. Cambridge University Press. https://doi.org/10.1017/9781108766425.

Guillén-Nieto, V., & Stein, D. (2022). Introduction: Theory and practice in forensic linguistics. In V. Guillen-Nieto & D. Stein (Eds.), *Language as evidence: Doing forensic linguistics* (pp. 1–33). Springer. https://doi.org/10.1007/978-3-030-84330-4_1.

Hadiyani, T. (2014). Tipe pertanyaan, respon dan praanggapan yang muncul pada interviu investigatif kepolisian. *PAROLE: Journal of Linguistics and Education*, 4(1), 38–53. https://ejournal.undip.ac.id/index.php/parole/article/view/6861.

Hale, S. (2011). The need to raise the bar: Court interpreters as specialised experts. *Judicial Review (Sydney, N.S.W.)*, 10(2), 237–258. https://search.informit.org/doi/10.3316/agispt.20112165.

Hale, S., Goodman-Delahunty, J., & Martschuk, N. (2019). Interpreter performance in police interviews. Differences between trained interpreters and untrained bilinguals. *The Interpreter and Translator Trainer*, 13(2), 107–131. https://doi.org/10.1080/1750399X.2018.1541649.

Halid, R. (2022). Tindak tutur pelaku pencemaran nama baik di media sosial: Kajian linguistik forensik. *KREDO: Jurnal Ilmiah Bahasa Dan Sastra*, 5(2), 441–458. https://doi.org/10.24176/kredo.v5i2.6342.

Hartoyo, H., Sindung, H., Teuku, F., & Sunarto, S. (2020). The role of local communities in peacebuilding in post-ethnic conflict in a multi-cultural society. *Journal of Aggression, Conflict and Peace Research*, 12(1), 33–44. https://doi.org/10.1108/JACPR-06-2019-0419.

Haryanto, & Arimi, S. (2022). The implication of the meaning of utterances in defamation cases: A forensic linguistics study. *Seloka: Jurnal Pendidikan Bahasa Dan Sastra Indonesia*, 11(1), 19–30.

Hatoum, B. (2023, November 4). *Historic breakthrough on investigative interviewing in Indonesia*. Norwegian Centre for Human Rights, University of Oslo.

Hendrokumoro, H., Masrukhi, M., D., L. S., & Laksanti, I. D. K. T. A. (2019). Peran linguistik forensik pada era perkembangan teknologi komunikasi. *Bakti Budaya*, 2(2), 81. https://doi.org/10.22146/bb.50961.

Hermawan, R., Rahyono, F. X., & Dallyono, R. (2021). Counter-claiming for a crime narrative: An evaluation of the defendant's plea at the corruption criminal court. *Indonesian Journal of Applied Linguistics*, 11(1), 167–176. https://doi.org/10.17509/ijal.v11i1.34669.

Heryanto, A. (1995, September 25). Permadi dan saksi ahli. *Forum Keadilan Nomor 12 Tahun IV*, 69. https://arielheryanto.com/wp-content/uploads/2016/02/1995_09_25_fk-permadi-dan-saksi-ahli-c1.pdf.

Heydon, G. (2014). Forensic linguistics: Forms and processes. *Linguistik Indonesia*, 32(1), 1–10. https://doi.org/10.26499/li.v32i1.11.

Human Rights Watch. (2010). *Turning critics into criminals: The human rights consequences of criminal defamation law in Indonesia*. www.hrw.org/sites/default/files/reports/indonesia0510webwcover.pdf.

Hutton, C. (2009). *Language, meaning, and the law*. Edinburgh University Press.

Ilzam, M. (2019). Revealing motives and language behavior in a suicide note. *IDEAS: Journal on English Language Teaching and Learning, Linguistics and Literature*, 7(1), 178–187. https://doi.org/10.24256/ideas.v7i1.737.

Inderasari, E., Kusno, A., & Kusmanto, H. (2022). A cultural-based mediation to solve defamation cases: A forensic linguistic study. *LiNGUA: Jurnal Ilmu Bahasa Dan Sastra*, 17(1), 73–84. https://doi.org/10.18860/ling.v17i1.13341.

Infotek HPI. (2024, August 1). *Rilis pelaksanaan Tes Sertifikasi Nasional (TSN) juru bahasa Himpunan Penerjemah Indonesia (HPI) tahun 2024*. Himpunan

Penerjemah Indonesia (HPI). www.hpi.or.id/rilis-pelaksanaan-tsn-juru-bahasa-hpi-tahun-2024.

Isra, S., & Tegnan, H. (2021). Legal syncretism or the theory of unity in diversity as an alternative to legal pluralism in Indonesia. *International Journal of Law and Management*, 63(6), 553–568. https://doi.org/10.1108/IJLMA-04-2018-0082.

Judiasih, S. D., & Fakhriah, E. L. (2018). Inheritance law system: Considering the pluralism of customary law in Indonesia. *PADJADJARAN Jurnal Ilmu Hukum (Journal of Law)*, 5(2), 315–330. https://doi.org/10.22304/pjih.v5n2.a6.

Karenisa, K. (2020). Penghinaan terhadap simbol dan pejabat negara dalam kajian linguistik forensik. *Telaga Bahasa*, 7(1), 55–72. https://doi.org/10.36843/tb.v7i1.57.

Khatimah, H., & Kusumawardani, F. (2016). Pedoman kajian linguistik forensik. In *Badan Pembinaan dan Pengembangan Bahasa*. Badan Pengembangan dan Pembinaan Bahasa.

Kniffka, H. (1996). On forensic linguistic "differential diagnosis." In H. Kniffka, S. Blackwell, & M. Coulthard (Eds.), *Recent developments in forensic linguistics* (pp. 75–122). Peter Lang Group AG.

Kniffka, H. (2007). *Working in language and law*. Palgrave Macmillan. https://doi.org/10.1057/9780230590045.

Kniffka, H. (2015). Applied (forensic) linguistics in in autochthonic and allochthonic use. In L. M. Solan, J. Ainsworth, & R. W. Shuy (Eds.), *Speaking of language and law: Conversations on the work of Peter Tiersma* (pp. 251–254). Oxford University Press.

Koagouw, M. O. (2022, June 1). *Suka duka Wayan Ana 35 tahun jadi penerjemah WNA di pengadilan*. DetikBali. www.detik.com/bali/berita/d-6105042/suka-duka-wayan-ana-35-tahun-jadi-penerjemah-wna-di-pengadilan.

Kurzon, D. (1997). 'Legal language': Varieties, genres, registers, discourses. *International Journal of Applied Linguistics*, 7(2), 119–139. https://doi.org/10.1111/j.1473-4192.1997.tb00111.x.

Kusno, A. (2021). Analisis wacana kritis model Fairclough sebagai alternatif pendekatan analisis kasus hukum dugaan pencemaran nama baik (kajian linguistik forensik). *Jurnal Forensik Kebahasaan*, 1(2), 134–161. https://ojs.badanbahasa.kemdikbud.go.id/jurnal/index.php/jfk/article/view/4443/1713.

Kusumanegara, A., Syihabuddin, Sudana, D., & Saifullah, A. R. (2022). Cultural confession in Indonesian religious courts: A forensic linguistics analysis. *European Online Journal of Natural and Social Sciences*, 11(3), 827–836. https://european-science.com/eojnss/article/view/6502.

Kusumawardani, F., & Puspitasari, D. A. (2021). Analisis attitude dalam per-undungan siber pada pelajar di Indonesia. *Jurnal Forensik Kebahasaan*, 1(2), 162–177. https://ojs.badanbahasa.kemdikbud.go.id/jurnal/index.php/jfk/article/view/4444.

Lai, M. (2016). Police cognitive interviews conducted through interpreters – an experimental study of the inherent conflicts in interlingual operations [RMIT University]. In *School of Global, Urban and Social Studies*. http://researchbank.rmit.edu.au/view/rmit:162065.

LBH Masyarakat. (2009, June). Wrong diagnosis: The case of Prita Mulyasari and the threat to free speech. *Caveat*, 3–7. http://indonesia.ahrchk.net/docs/CaveatV01-I.pdf.

Levi, J. N. (1994). Language as evidence: The linguist as expert witness in North American courts. *The International Journal of Speech, Language and the Law*, 1(1), 1–26.

Liu, A. H., & Ricks, J. I. (2022). *Ethnicity and politics in Southeast Asia*. Cambridge University Press. https://doi.org/10.1017/9781108933179.

Longhi, J., & Makouar, N. (2025). New challenges in forensic and legal linguistics. MDPI *MDM*. https://doi.org/10.3390/BOOKS978-3-7258-3932-2.

Lopes, G. (2024). Artificial intelligence and judicial decision-making: Evaluating the role of AI in debiasing. *Journal for Technology Assessment in Theory and Practice*, *33*, 28–33. https://doi.org/10.14512/tatup.33.1.28.

Lubis, Y. B. S., Sinar, T. S., & Masdiana, L. (2023). Question and respond types in courtroom: A forensic linguistics analysis. *LingPoet: Journal of Linguistics and Literary Research*, 4(2), 127–138. https://talenta.usu.ac.id/lingpoet/article/view/8769.

Lukito, R. (2012). *Legal pluralism in Indonesia*. Routledge. https://doi.org/10.4324/9780203113134.

Macleod, N., & Wright, D. (2020). Forensic linguistics. In S. Adolphs & D. Knight (Eds.), *The Routledge handbook of English language and digital humanities* (1st ed.). Routledge.

Mahsun. (2018). *Linguistik forensik: Memahami forensik berbasis teks dalam analogi DNA*. PT Rajagrafindo Persada.

Manik, S., Pardede, H., Franklin, T. N. D., & Pasaribu, T. K. A. (2022). Impoliteness in Indonesian hate speech on Basuki Tjahaja Purnama (BTP) as found in YouTube commentary. *Jurnal Education and Development*, 10(3), 420–429.

Mardikantoro, H. B., & Yuniawan, T. (2024). Cases of women's hate speech due to the use of taboo language on social media. *Theory and Practice in Language Studies*, 14(9), 2814–2822. https://doi.org/10.17507/tpls.1409.17.

Margiyono. (2010). *Seri reformasi kebijakan media seri II: Kasus pencemaran nama baik.* https://aji.or.id/upload/article_doc/Kasus_Pencemaran_Nama.pdf.

Marlia, M., Lukmana, I., & Gunawan, W. (2023). Contesting Indonesian plain vs legal languages: Analysis of effectiveness on Indonesian controversial law. *Theory and Practice in Language Studies*, 13(5), 1217–1225. https://doi.org/10.17507/tpls.1305.16.

McMenamin, G. R. (2002). *Forensic linguistics: Advances in forensic stylistics.* CRC Press, Taylor & Francis Group.

Meliala, A. E. (2001). The notion of sensitivity in policing. *International Journal of the Sociology of Law*, 29(2), 99–111. https://doi.org/10.1006/ijsl.2001.0144.

Mintowati. (2016). Pencemaran nama baik: Kajian linguistik forensik. *Paramasastra Jurnal Ilmiah Bahasa, Sastra Dan Pembelajarannya*, 3(2), 197–208. https://journal.unesa.ac.id/index.php/paramasastra/article/view/1525/1040.

Mira, S. (2002, October). Seorang ahli linguistik bisa memperingan kerja hakim. *ISOLA Pos*.

Mubarok, Y., Sudana, D., Yanti, D., Aisyah, A. D., & Af'idah, A. N. (2024). Abusive comments (hate speech) on Indonesian social media: A forensic linguistics approach. *Theory and Practice in Language Studies*, 14(5), 1440–1449. https://doi.org/10.17507/tpls.1405.16.

Muniroh, R. D. D. (2019). "It's better to see a tiger than a police officer": Adapting the cognitive interviewing technique to the Indonesian policing context [RMIT University]. In *School of Global, Urban and Social Studies: Vol. PhD*. https://researchbank.rmit.edu.au/view/rmit:162708.

Muniroh, R. D. D., & Aziz, E. A. (2016). The contemporary practices of Indonesian police interviewing of witnesses. In D. Walsh, G. E. Oxburgh, A. D. Redlich, & T. Myklebust (Eds.), *International developments and practices in investigative interviewing and interrogation Volume 1: Victims and witnesses* (pp. 7–18). Routledge.

Muniroh, R. D. D., Findling, J., & Heydon, G. (2018). What's in a question: A case for a culturally appropriate interviewing protocol in the Australian Refugee Review Tribunal. In I. Nick (Ed.), *Forensic linguistics, asylum seekers, refugees and immigrants* (pp. 133–154). Vernon Press.

Muniroh, R. D. D., & Heydon, G. (2022). Addressing the gap between principles and practices in police interviewing in Indonesia. *Journal of Police and Criminal Psychology*, 37(2), 312–324. https://doi.org/10.1007/s11896-021-09474-7.

Muniroh, R. D. D., & Heydon, G. (2024). The efficacy of the Delphi method for adapting cognitive interviewing instructions into culturally and linguistically diverse international policing contexts. *International Journal of Speech, Language and the Law*, 31(1), 131–153. https://doi.org/10.1558/ijsll.24367.

Muniroh, R. D. D., Sukma, B. P., Puspitasari, D. A. et al. (2022). *Arena perundungan siber: Menelusuri benih-benih kebencian di media sosial* (R. D. D. Muniroh (ed.)). Deepublish.

Mutaqin, Z. Z. (2011). Indonesian customary law and European colonialism: A comparative analysis on adat law. *JE Asia & Int'l L*, 4, 351.

Na'im, A & Syaputra, H. (2011). Kewarganegaraan, suku bangsa, agama, dan Bahasa Sehari-hari Penduduk Indonesia Hasil Sensus Penduduk 2010. Jakarta: Badan Pusat Statistik.

Ng, E. (2023). The right to a fair trial and the right to interpreting. *Interpreting: International Journal of Research and Practice in Interpreting*, 25(1), 87–108. https://doi.org/10.1075/intp.00082.ng.

Olsson, J. (2008). *Forensic linguistics: Second edtion*. London: Continuum International Publishing Group.

Olsson, J., & Luchjenbroers, J. (2014). *Forensic linguistics*. Bloomsbury.

Pastika, I. W. (2019). Dugaan blasfemi dalam puisi "Ibu Indonesia": Analisis linguistik forensik. *Osaka University Knowledge Archive*, 2, 15–28. https://ir.library.osaka-u.ac.jp/repo/ouka/all/71879/ffle_02_015.pdf.

Pastika, I. W., Dewi, E. P. S., & Putra, I. B. G. D. (2023). Language cases against UU ITE in Indonesia. *International Journal of Linguistics, Literature and Culture*, 9(5), 198–208. https://doi.org/10.21744/ijllc.v9n5.2361.

Pastika, I. W., & Puspani, I. A. M. (2021). *Linguistik forensik: Studi kasus teks lintas bahasa*. Pustaka Larasan. https://books.google.com/books/about/Linguistik_forensik.html?id=VNy4zgEACAAJ.

Pavlenko, A. (2024). Language proficiency as a matter of law: Judicial reasoning on Miranda waivers by speakers with Limited English Proficiency (LEP). *International Journal for the Semiotics of Law – Revue Internationale de Sémiotique Juridique*, 37(2), 329–357. https://doi.org/10.1007/s11196-023-10037-8.

Perkins, R. C. (2021). The application of forensic linguistics in cybercrime investigations. *Policing: A Journal of Policy and Practice*, 15(1), 68–78. https://doi.org/10.1093/police/pay097.

Pratama, H. A., & Ibrahim, F. (2024, June 27). *Police reported as perpetrators of most torture acts in Indonesia: Komnas HAM, KontraS, Tempo.Co*. Tempo.Co.

Priambodo, B. B. (2018). Positioning adat law in the Indonesia's legal system: Historical discourse and current development on customary law. *Udayana*

Journal of Law and Culture, 2(2), 140. https://doi.org/10.24843/UJLC.2018 .v02.i02.p02.

Purnama, S. (2023). Pragmatic analysis of verbal attacks in Indonesian courtrooms: Exploring prevalence, nature, and cultural influences. *Indonesian Journal of Applied Linguistics*, 13(2), 418–429. https://doi.org/10.17509/ ijal.v13i2.63095.

Puspitasari, D. A. (2022). Corpus-based speech act analysis on the use of word "lu" in cyberbullying speech. *Proceedings of the 1st Konferensi Internasional Berbahasa Indonesia Universitas Indraprasta PGRI, KIBAR 2020, 28 October 2020, Jakarta, Indonesia*. https://doi.org/10.4108/eai.28- 10-2020.2315314.

Puspitasari, D. A., Fakhrurroja, H., & Sutrisno, A. (2023). Identify fake author in Indonesia crime cases: A forensic authorship analysis using N-gram and stylometric features. *2023 International Conference on Advancement in Data Science, E-Learning and Information System (ICADEIS)*, 1–6. https://doi .org/10.1109/ICADEIS58666.2023.10271069.

Puspitasari, D. A., Fakhrurroja, H., & Sutrisno, A. (2024). Authorship analysis in electronic texts using similarity comparison method. *Linguistik Indonesia*, 42(1), 91–112. https://doi.org/10.26499/li.v42i1.544.

Puspitasari, D. A., Sutrisno, A., & Fakhrurroja, H. (2025). N-gram based authorship analysis in Indonesian text: Evidence case study in authorship dispute cases. In R. Stroupe & L. Roosman (Eds.), *Applied Linguistics in the Indonesian Contexts* (pp. 181–198). Springer.

Radfar, Z. H., Sudana, D., & Gunawan, W. (2020). Gricean maxim violation(s) in the murder case of Jamal Khashoggi. *NOBEL: Journal of Literature and Language Teaching*, 11(2), 162–177. https://doi.org/10.15642/ NOBEL.2020.11.2.162-177.

Rahardjo, S. (1994). Between two worlds: Modern state and traditional society in Indonesia. *Law & Society Review*, 28(3), 493–502. https://doi.org/10.2307/ 3054068.

Ramadani, R., Syaifullah, A. R., Gunawan, W. et al. (2023). Implicature and question types of police interrogation: An analysis of communication in a theft case. *World Journal of English Language*, 13(7), 585. https://doi.org/ 10.5430/wjel.v13n7p585.

Raspati, L. (2012). Keberadaan ahli dan implikasi negatifnya terhadap asas peradilan cepat, sederhana dan biaya ringan (suatu kritik terhadap pemeriksaan ahli dalam peradilan pidana di Indonesia. *Negara Hukum*, 3(2), 249– 273.

Rasyid, A., Lubis, R. F., Hutagalung, M. W. R. et al. (2023). Local wisdom recognition in inter-ethnic religious conflict resolution in Indonesia from

Islah perspective. *JURIS (Jurnal Ilmiah Syariah)*, 22(1), 13. https://doi.org/10.31958/juris.v22i1.8432.

Ria, R. N., & Setiawan, T. (2023). Forensic linguistic analysis of netizens' hate speech acts in Tik-Tok comment section. *Britain International of Linguistics Arts and Education (BIoLAE) Journal*, 5(2), 141–152. https://doi.org/10.33258/biolae.v5i2.894.

Ridhwani, N. H., & Sawirman, S. (2020). The process type and participant function of Jiah Khan's, Kevin Carter's, and Virginia Woolf's suicide discourses. *Andalas International Journal of Socio-Humanities*, 2(1), 22–29. https://doi.org/10.25077/aijosh.v2i1.11.

Rifai, H. A. (2020). *"This Bill is Liberal!": An Investigation into the Issue of Linguistic Ambiguity in the Indonesian Sexual Violence Bill*. Cardiff University.

Rifki, Y., Sawirman, & Usman, F. (2021). Transitivity analysis in detecting fraudulent language in email: Forensic linguistics approach. *IJOTL-TL: Indonesian Journal of Language Teaching and Linguistics*, 6(1), 30–41.

Rosili, N. A. K., Zakaria, N. H., Hassan, R. et al. (2020). A systematic literature review of machine learning methods in predicting court decisions. *International Journal of Artificial Intelligence*, 8, 31–42.

Rossner, M., Tait, D., & McCurdy, M. (2021). Justice reimagined: Challenges and opportunities with implementing virtual courts. *Current Issues in Criminal Justice*, 33(1), 94–110. https://doi.org/10.1080/10345329.2020.1859968.

Rustandi, A. (2011, October 10). *UPI Bandung kembangkan bidang forensik linguistik*. Inilah.Com. www.inilah.com/upi-bandung-kembangkan-bidang-forensik-linguistik.

Safitra, Z., Saifullah, A. R., & Syihabuddin, S. (2024). Analysis of the illocutionary force of a stalker in "Can I tell you a secret?" A forensic linguistics perspective. *Wiralodra English Journal*, 8(2), 214–224. https://doi.org/10.31943/wej.v8i2.308.

Saifullah, A. R. (2021, November). Linguistik forensik pada era digital: Analisis SWOT dan implikasi teoretis, metodologis dan praktis. *Seminar Daring Linguistik Forensik Pada Era Digital*.

Salahuddin, M., Ahmad, A., Suharti, S., Syukri, S., & Nurhilaliati, N. (2023). Between adat law and national law: The resistance of Sasak women to their inheritance rights in Lombok Indonesia. *Lex Localis – Journal of Local Self-Government*, 21(4), 923–936. https://doi.org/10.4335/21.4.923-936(2023).

Santoso, D., & Apriyanto, S. (2020). Pragmatics implicature analysis of police interrogation: Forensic linguistics analysis. *International Journal of Psychosocial Rehabilitation*, 24(6), 115–124.

Sanubarianto, S. T., Sitanggang, N. P., Hendrastuti, R. et al. (2023). Swear words from the transgender lexicon in the hate speech law case in Indonesia. *Proceedings of the 3rd International Conference on Linguistics and Cultural (ICLC 2022)*, 172–180. https://doi.org/10.2991/978-2-38476-070-1_15.

Sarifuddin, S., Tadjuddin, M., & Iswary, E. (2021). A hate and provocative speech act in social media: A forensic linguistics study. *ELS Journal on Interdisciplinary Studies in Humanities*, 4(3), 363–368. https://doi.org/10.34050/elsjish.v4i3.18196.

Satria, H., Darwis, M., & Kamsinah. (2022). Implikatur percakapan interogasi terhadap saksi/korban penganiyaan: Kajian linguistik forensik. *Jurnal Ilmu Budaya*, 10(2), 18–25.

Dharmaraj, S. (2024). Indonesia: AI and digital tools in forensic linguistics [online]. Open Gov Asia. Available from: https://opengovasia.com/2024/11/19/indonesia-ai-and-digital-tools-in-forensic-linguistics/ [Accessed 26 Dec 2024].

Sawirman, S., Hadi, N., & Yusdi, M. (2014). *Linguistik forensik Volume 1*. Pusat Studi Ketahanan Nasional Universitas Andalas. http://repo.unand.ac.id/49633/1/Linguistik Forensik Volume 1 sent Repo.pdf.

Sawirman, Hadi, N., & Yusdi, M. (2015). *Linguistik forensik Volume 2*. Pusat Studi Ketahanan Nasional Universitas Andalas. http://repo.unand.ac.id/49632/2/Linguistik Forensik Volume 2 2015-ok.pdf.

Searle, J. R. (1969). *Speech acts: An essay in the philosophy of language.* Cambridge University Press.

Shidarta, S. (2017). Laws of language and legal language: A study of legal language in some Indonesian regulations. *Humaniora*, 8(1), 97. https://doi.org/10.21512/humaniora.v8i1.3700.

Sholihatin, E. (2019). *Linguistik forensik dan kejahatan berbahasa.* Pustaka Pelajar.

Shuy, R. W. (2000). Breaking into language and law: The trials of the insider-linguist. In J. E. Alatis, H. E. Hamilton, & A. Tan (Eds.), *Linguistics, Language, and the Professions: Education, Journalism, Law, Medicine, and Technology* (pp. 67–80). Georgetown University Press.

Shuy, R. W. (2006). *Linguistics in the courtroom: A practical guide.* Oxford University Press.

Shuy, R. W. (2008). *Fighting over words: Language and civil law cases.* Oxford University Press.

Shuy, R. W. (2017). Language and law. In M. Aronoff & J. Rees-Miller (Eds.), *The handbook of linguistics* (2nd ed., pp. 627–643). John Wiley & Sons. https://doi.org/10.1002/9781119072256.ch31.

Shuy, R. W. (2021). How I got started as a forensic linguist. *Language and Law/ Linguagem e Direito*, 7(1–2), 8–11. https://ojs.letras.up.pt/index.php/LLLD/ article/view/10340.

Simarmata, R. (2019). The enforceability of formalised customary land rights in Indonesia. . *Australian Journal of Asian Law*, 19(2), 299–313.

Sinaga, L. C., Kusumaningtyas, A. N., & Rozi, S. (2024). "Tionghoa" or Cina': Negotiating Chinese-Indonesians' preferred identity in the post-reform era. *Asian Ethnicity*, 25(2), 340–366. https://doi.org/10.1080/14631369.2023 .2257615.

Sinar, T. S., Zein, T. T., & Nurlela. (2021). Attitude analysis in courtroom discourse by using English systemic functional linguistics. *Asian EFL Journal*, 28(3), 75–86. www.asian-efl-journal.com/monthly-editions-new/ 2021-monthly-edition/volume-28-issue-3-3-june-2021/index.htm.

Sirulhaq, A., Yuwono, U., & Muta'ali, A. (2023). Why do we need a socio-cognitive-CDA in hate speech studies? A corpus-based systematic review. *Discourse & Society*, 34(4), 462–484. https://doi.org/10.1177/0957926522 1126599.

Sofyan, R., & Rosa, R. N. (2021). Problems and strategies in translating legal texts. *Humanus*, 20(2), 221. https://doi.org/10.24036/humanus.v20i2.112233.

Solan, L. M. (2005). *The language of judges*. University of Chicago Press.

Solan, L. M. (2010). *The language of statutes: Laws and their interpretation*. Chicago University Press.

Steinhauer, H. (1994). The Indonesian language situation and linguistics: Prospects and possibilities. *Bijdragen Tot de Taal-, Land- En Volkenkunde*, 150(IV), 755–784. https://doi.org/10.1163/22134379-90003070.

Subuki, M., Nuryani, Sholeha, M., Hudaa, S., & Hariyanto, B. (2023). Konstruksi argumentasi putusan Pengadilan Negeri Gunung Sitoli No. 07/ Pid.B/2013/PN-GS: Kajian linguistik forensik. *KEMBARA Journal of Scientific Language Literature and Teaching*, 9(1), 89–102. https://doi.org/ 10.22219/kembara.v9i1.24279.

Subyantoro. (2022). *Linguistik forensik: Sebuah pengantar*. CV Farishma Indonesia.

Subyantoro, S., Zuliyanti, Z., & Putri, S. F. D. (2023). Impoliteness strategy for cyberbullying in Indonesian on Instagram social media. *KEMBARA Journal of Scientific Language Literature and Teaching*, 9(2), 735–749. https://doi .org/10.22219/kembara.v9i2.25517.

Sujatna, E. T. S., & Sujatna, M. L. (2020). Processes in Kurt Cobain's suicide note. *IJFL (International Journal of Forensic Linguistics)*, 1(1), 1–9. www .ejournal.warmadewa.ac.id/index.php/ijfl/article/view/1658.

Sukma, B. P., Hendrastuti, R., Rahmawati, A. et al. (2023). *Hukum dalam teroka linguistik* (N. P. Sitanggang (ed.)). Penerbit BRIN. https://doi.org/10.55981/brin.737.

Sukma, B. P., Puspitasari, D. A., Afiyani, S. A. et al. (2021). Cyberbullying speech patterns among Indonesian students. *Jurnal Bahasa Dan Seni*, 49(2), 205–223. https://doi.org/10.17977/um015v49i22021p205.

Suryani, Y., Istianingrum, R., & Hanik, S. U. (2021). Linguistik forensik ujaran kebencian terhadap artis Aurel Hermansyah di media sosial Instagram. *BELAJAR BAHASA: Jurnal Ilmiah Program Studi Pendidikan Bahasa Dan Sastra Indonesia*, 6(1), 107–118. https://doi.org/10.32528/bb.v6i1.4167.

Suryasa, W., Wirawan, I. G. N., Thoms, S. L., & Bonviglio, T. (2021). Legal terms in translation of regulation number 40 year 2007 regarding limited liability company in Indonesia. *Linguistics and Culture Review*, 6(1), 30–42. https://doi.org/10.21744/lingcure.v6n1.1731.

Susanto, Zhenhua, W., Yingli, W., & Nanda, D. S. (2017). Forensic linguistic inquiry into the validity of F0 as discriminatory potential in the system of forensic speaker verification. *Journal of Forensic Sciences & Criminal Investigation*, 5(3), 1–8. https://doi.org/10.19080/JFSCI.2017.05.555664.

Svartvik, J. (1968). *The Evans statements: A case for forensic linguistics.* University of Goteburg.

Svennevig, J., Urbanik, P., & Diepeveen, A. (2024). How police investigators seek to secure that suspects speaking a second language understand their rights in investigative interviews. *Police Practice and Research*, 25(3), 324–342. https://doi.org/10.1080/15614263.2023.2233660.

Syahid, A., Sudana, D., & Bachari, A. D. (2021, December). Hate speech and blasphemy on social media in Indonesia: Forensic linguistic studies. *Proceedings of the International Congress of Indonesian Linguistics Society (KIMLI 2021)*. https://doi.org/10.2991/assehr.k.211226.001.

Syahid, A., Sudana, D., & Bachari, A. D. (2022). Perundungan siber (cyberbullying) bermuatan penistaan agama di media sosial yang berdampak hukum: Kajian linguistik forensik. *Semantik*, 11(1), 17–32. https://doi.org/10.22460/semantik.v11i1.p17-32.

Tamma, S., & Duile, T. (2020). Indigeneity and the state in Indonesia: The local turn in the dialectic of recognition. *Journal of Current Southeast Asian Affairs*, 39(2), 270–289. https://doi.org/10.1177/1868103420905967.

Tampubolon, E. C. (2024). Unfair access to justice for non-Indonesian speakers. *Dialogia Iuridica*, 16(1), 112–141. https://doi.org/10.28932/di.v16i1.10039.

Tarigan, S. N., & Mulyadi. (2019). Forensic linguistics: Ratna Sarumpaet's persecution case on hate speech. *International Journal of Linguistics, Literature and Translation (IJLLT)*, 2(1), 168–175. https://media.neliti

.com/media/publications/290228-forensic-linguistics-ratna-sarumpaets-pe-bc45aee5.pdf.

Tayebi, T., & Coulthard, M. (2022). New trends in forensic linguistics. *Language and Law=Linguagem e Direito*, 9(1), 1–8. https://doi.org/10.21747/21833745/lanlaw/9_1ed.

Teguh, I. (2019, July 2). *Mochtar Lubis: Pembangkang dua rezim yang tak gentar berpolemik.* https://tirto.id/mochtar-lubis-pembangkang-dua-rezim-yang-tak-gentar-berpolemik-edqg.

Thalib, M. C. (2023). Implications of mixed marriage in the perspective of Gorontalo customary law and its reality based on International Private Law principles. *Jambura Law Review*, 5(1), 179–198. https://doi.org/10.33756/jlr.v5i1.16798.

Thamrin, H., Sudana, D., Bachari, A. D., & Muniroh, R. D. D. (2023). Fake news analysis of Supreme Court decision from forensic linguistics and critical discourse analysis perspectives. *Journal of English Education and Teaching*, 7(4), 847–861. https://doi.org/10.33369/jeet.7.4.847-861.

Tiersma, P. M. (1993). Review: Linguistic issues in the law. *Language*, 69(1), 113–137. https://doi.org/10.2307/416418.

Tiersma, P. M. (1999). *Legal language.* The University of Chicago Press.

Tiersma, P. M. (2008). The nature of legal Language. In J. Gibbons & M. T. Turell (Eds.), *Dimensions of forensic linguistics* (pp. 7–25). John Benjamins.

Tiwisia, V., Maroni, M., & Tisnanto, H. . (2023). Problems of virtual criminal trials in Indonesia's criminal justice system. *Remittances Review*, 8(4), 3554–3562.

Toan, L. N. (2024). The role of language in ensuring logical and reasonable presentation in legal texts. *Revista de Gestão Social e Ambiental*, 18(4), e06706. https://doi.org/10.24857/rgsa.v18n4-126.

Toulmin, Stephen. (2003). *The uses of argument.* Cambridge University Press.

Tracy, K. (2024). Preliminary jury instructing: A dilemmatic communication practice. *Text & Talk*, 44(2), 271–291. https://doi.org/10.1515/text-2021-0115.

Utami, P. (2020, October 16). *Why so serious?* Inside Indonesia. www.insideindonesia.org/archive/articles/why-so-serious#:~:text=Anjayisacolloquialversion,happiness%2Cshock%2Canddisappointment.

Van Leeuwen, T. (2004). *Discourse and technology:Multimodal discourse analysis.* Springer.

Vidhiasi, D. M., Muniroh, R. D. D., Gunawan, W. et al. (2024). Person reference in police interviews: A case study of domestic violence in Indonesia. *Indonesian Journal of Applied Linguistics*, 13(3), 490–499. https://doi.org/10.17509/ijal.v13i3.66954.

Wardhani, L. T. A. L., Noho, M. D. H., & Natalis, A. (2022). The adoption of various legal systems in Indonesia: An effort to initiate the prismatic mixed legal systems. *Cogent Social Sciences*, 8(1), 1–21. https://doi.org/10.1080/23311886.2022.2104710.

Warman, K., Isra, S., & Tegnan, H. (2018). Enhancing legal pluralism: The role of adat and Islamic laws within the Indonesian legal system. *Journal of Legal, Ethical and Regulatory Issues*, 21(3), 1.

Widiantho, Y. (2020). Hate speech addressed to President Joko Widodo in online media: Impoliteness strategies analysis. *LingPoet: Journal of Linguistics and Literary Research*, 1(1), 14–19. https://doi.org/10.32734/lingpoet.v1i1.4692.

Wijaya, A. R., & Rizal, C. A. (2023). Social discrimination: A case study of social subordination to Eastern Vernacular Indonesian speakers. *PRASASTI: Journal of Linguistics*, 8(1), 1. https://doi.org/10.20961/prasasti.v8i1.59278.

Woodman, G. R. (1999). The idea of legal pluralism. In B. Dupret, M. Berger, & L. Al-Zwaini (Eds.), *Legal pluralism in the Arab world* (pp. 3–19). Brill.

Wright, D., & Picornell, I. (2024). Semiotic perspectives on forensic and legal linguistics: Unifying approaches in the language of the legal process and language in evidence. *International Journal for the Semiotics of Law – Revue Internationale de Sémiotique Juridique*, 37, 293–304. https://doi.org/10.1007/s11196-023-10094-z.

Yi, R. (2024). Justice under microscope: Analysing Mandarin Chinese markers in virtual courtroom discourse. *Discourse Studies*, 26(1), 117–135. https://doi.org/10.1177/14614456231197045.

Yoserwan. (2024). Implications of adat criminal law incorporation into the new Indonesian Criminal Code: Strengthening or weakening? *Cogent Social Sciences*, 10(1), 1, 1–11. https://doi.org/10.1080/23311886.2023.2289599.

Yulia, R., Prakarsa, A., & Bustami, M. R. (2023). Harmonizing adat obligations and state law: A case study of murder and rape cases in Baduy's Indonesia. *Journal of Indonesian Legal Studies*, 8(2), 803–854. https://doi.org/10.15294/jils.v8i2.72283.

Yusuf, Y. Q., Mansur, T. M., & Muthalib, K. A. (2024). Language to contest legitimacy: The acceptability of Qanun Putroe Phang in light of the Acehnese discourse. *Training, Language and Culture*, 8(3), 52–61. https://doi.org/10.22363/2521-442X-2024-8-3-52-61.

Zein, S. (2020). *Language policy in superdiverse Indonesia*. Routledge.

Zifana, M., Lukmana, I., & Sudana, D. (2021). The portrayal of defamation case defendant in court verdict. *Indonesian Journal of Applied Linguistics*, 11(1), 94–103. https://doi.org/10.17509/ijal.v11i1.34672.

Zulaeha, I., Yuiawan, T., Suproyono, A. Y., Wijayanti, H., & Prihatmini, E. (2022). The humanist expressive speech acts of the judicial panel at the state court. *Proceedings of the 6th International Conference on Science, Education and Technology (ISET 2020)*. https://doi.org/10.2991/assehr .k.211125.091.

Acknowledgments

The authors express their gratitude to the Series Editors for their guidance, the anonymous reviewers for their constructive feedback, and all survey participants for their valuable contributions. Appreciation is also due to Rizki Juanda for assistance with literature data collection and analysis. The use of artificial intelligence tools for language refinement is acknowledged.

Forensic Linguistics

Tim Grant
Aston University

Tim Grant is Professor of Forensic Linguistics, Director of the Aston Institute for Forensic Linguistics, and past president of the International Association of Forensic Linguists. His recent publications have focussed on online sexual abuse conversations including *Language and Online Identities: The Undercover Policing of Internet Sexual Crime* (with Nicci MacLeod, Cambridge, 2020).

Tim is one of the world's most experienced forensic linguistic practitioners and his case work has involved the analysis of abusive and threatening communications in many different contexts including investigations into sexual assault, stalking, murder, and terrorism. He also makes regular media contributions including presenting police appeals such as for the BBC Crimewatch programme.

Tammy Gales
Hofstra University

Tammy Gales is Professor of Linguistics and the Director of Research at the Institute for Forensic Linguistics, Threat Assessment, and Strategic Analysis at Hofstra University, New York. She has served on the Executive Committee for the International Association of Forensic Linguists (IAFL), is on the editorial board for the peer-reviewed journals Applied Corpus Linguistics and Language and Law / Linguagem e Direito, and is a member of the advisory board for the BYU Law and Corpus Linguistics group. Her research interests cross the boundaries of forensic linguistics and language and the law, with a primary focus on threatening communications. She has trained law enforcement agents from agencies across Canada and the U.S. and has applied her work to both criminal and civil cases.

About the Series

Elements in Forensic Linguistics provides high-quality accessible writing, bringing cutting-edge forensic linguistics to students and researchers as well as to practitioners in law enforcement and law. Elements in the series range from descriptive linguistics work, documenting a full range of legal and forensic texts and contexts; empirical findings and methodological developments to enhance research, investigative advice, and evidence for courts; and explorations into the theoretical and ethical foundations of research and practice in forensic linguistics.

For EU product safety concerns, contact us at Calle de José Abascal, 56–1°, 28003 Madrid, Spain or eugpsr@cambridge.org.